Industrial IoT Security: Protecting Smart Factories and SCADA Systems

Zephyrion Stravos

Introduction: Welcome to the Wild West of Industrial IoT Security

You ever walk into a smart factory and feel like you just stepped onto the set of a sci-fi movie? The hum of robotic arms, conveyor belts that glide like they have minds of their own, sensors blinking with mysterious intent—it's mesmerizing. But if you've been in the cybersecurity game long enough, you also know something else: this entire cybernetic wonderland is one fat, juicy target waiting to be hacked.

That's right. Behind all the efficiency and automation lies a tangled mess of old-school industrial control systems duct-taped to modern IoT technology. It's like strapping a rocket engine to a horse-drawn carriage—sure, it moves fast, but you just know something's gonna explode. And if you're reading this, you're either A) trying to prevent that explosion, B) looking for ways to ethically cause that explosion (red teamers, I see you), or C) just really bad at picking bedtime stories.

Either way, welcome to "Industrial IoT Security: Protecting Smart Factories and SCADA Systems"—the next thrilling installment in my "IoT Red Teaming" series. If you've read my other books (and if you haven't, what are you even doing with your life?), you already know the drill. We're diving deep into how these systems work, how they break, and how to keep them from turning into the next cybersecurity dumpster fire.

Wait… Factories Can Be Hacked?

Oh, buddy. Not only can they be hacked, but they're some of the juiciest targets on the cyber battlefield. Industrial IoT (IIoT) is the backbone of modern manufacturing, powering everything from automated assembly lines to power grids, water treatment plants, and even nuclear facilities (yes, that kind of nuclear). But here's the kicker—these systems weren't originally built with security in mind. In fact, some of them still use default passwords from the 90s.

You think I'm joking?

There's an entire generation of factory engineers out there who have been doing things the same way since pagers were cool. That means critical systems still run on ancient Windows XP machines, hardcoded credentials, and protocols that are about as secure as a wet paper bag. It's like discovering a high-tech vault guarded by a wooden door with a "Do Not Enter" sign. And the bad guys? They know this.

The Attack Surface: Bigger Than You Think

When you hear "hacking," you probably think about some hoodie-wearing keyboard warrior cracking passwords in a dark room. But industrial hacking? Oh, it's way more creative than that. Here's just a taste of the delicious chaos that can unfold in a smart factory:

- **Ransomware Attack**: Wanna see a factory come to a screeching halt? Just encrypt a few PLCs (Programmable Logic Controllers, for the uninitiated), and suddenly, nobody's making car parts today.
- **Wireless Hijacking**: Zigbee, LoRa, 5G, RFID—if it transmits wirelessly, someone's trying to intercept it. And once they do? Let's just say you might find your assembly line suddenly manufacturing a lot of... nothing.
- **Firmware Tampering**: Ever wonder what happens when an industrial robot gets new "instructions" from an unexpected update? Yeah, neither did that auto manufacturer—until the cars coming off the line started having... creative design changes.
- **SCADA Manipulation**: If you don't know what SCADA is yet, don't worry—we'll get there. Just know that when someone messes with it, entire power grids and water supplies can go haywire. (Stuxnet, anyone?)

And that's just scratching the surface. We haven't even talked about air-gapped exploits, insider threats, and the absolute nightmare of legacy OT (Operational Technology) security.

IT vs. OT: The Never-Ending Battle

Speaking of OT, let's talk about the long-running turf war between IT (Information Technology) and OT (Operational Technology). IT folks live in a world of firewalls, endpoint protection, and SOC monitoring. OT engineers? They care about one thing: keeping the machines running.

If you ever want to witness pure chaos, put an IT security team in a room with an OT engineer and ask them how to patch a critical vulnerability. The IT guys will demand it be fixed immediately. The OT guys will stare at them like they just suggested replacing all the nuts and bolts in an airplane mid-flight.

Why? Because OT systems can't afford downtime. These machines run 24/7, and shutting them down just to apply some security patch isn't an option. So instead, vulnerabilities sit there, ripe for exploitation, while everyone prays nothing goes wrong. Spoiler alert: something always goes wrong.

The IoT Red Teaming Playbook

That's where this book—and the entire "IoT Red Teaming" series—comes in. Whether you're a security professional trying to lock things down or a penetration tester looking for your next challenge, you'll find plenty of battle-tested strategies here. And if you're new to the game? Well, congratulations—you're about to develop a healthy paranoia about the devices running our modern world.

This book is just one part of a much bigger hacking adventure. Maybe you started with "Firmware Hacking & Reverse Engineering", diving into the guts of embedded systems. Or perhaps "Wireless Hacking Unleashed" got you addicted to breaking radio signals (trust me, it happens). If cars are your thing, "The Car Hacker's Guide" probably got your engine running (pun intended).

And if you're feeling really ambitious? Well, "Satellite Hacking" is waiting for you to explore the final frontier of cybersecurity. (Yes, you can hack things in space. No, NASA does not appreciate it.)

What You'll Learn in This Book

In the chapters ahead, we'll break down Industrial IoT security piece by piece:

- How industrial networks are built (and how to break them).
- The real differences between IT and OT security (because they're like oil and water).
- The most common attack vectors in IIoT and SCADA systems (and how attackers exploit them).
- Defensive strategies that actually work (because hope is not a security strategy).
- The future of IIoT security—AI, blockchain, quantum computing, and all the fun chaos ahead.

Let's Get Started

Look, I'm not here to sugarcoat things—industrial security is a mess. But it's also one of the most important battlefronts in cybersecurity today. Whether you're a defender, an ethical hacker, or just someone trying to keep the lights on (literally), this book will give you the knowledge you need to navigate this chaotic world.

So, grab some coffee, maybe a tinfoil hat, and let's dive into the crazy, often terrifying, but always exciting world of Industrial IoT Security.

Trust me—you'll never look at a factory the same way again.

Chapter 1: Introduction to Industrial IoT (IIoT) Security

Picture this: You walk into a high-tech factory, robots zipping around, conveyor belts humming, and screens flashing data faster than your brain can process. It's a beautiful, synchronized dance of technology—until you realize half these machines are running on outdated firmware, default passwords, and security protocols weaker than your grandma's Wi-Fi password. Welcome to Industrial IoT (IIoT), where efficiency reigns supreme, and security? Well, that's often an afterthought—until something explodes (figuratively… hopefully).

This chapter introduces the fundamental concepts of Industrial IoT (IIoT) security, covering the architecture of smart factories, the convergence of IT (Information Technology) and OT (Operational Technology), and the unique challenges in securing industrial environments. We'll also explore key differences between IT and OT security, the growing attack surface in IIoT, and the most common threats facing modern industrial systems.

1.1 Understanding IIoT and Smart Factory Architectures

Welcome to the Future—Where Even Your Toaster is Smarter Than Your Firewall

Let's be real—when we imagined the future, we pictured flying cars, robotic assistants, and maybe a world where printers didn't randomly decide to ruin our day. Instead, we got smart factories, where industrial machines talk to each other, robots handle manufacturing, and sensors track everything from temperature to employee coffee breaks.

Welcome to the world of Industrial IoT (IIoT)—where automation meets cybersecurity nightmares. It's a game-changer for manufacturing, energy, and critical infrastructure, but like all great innovations, it also opens up a Pandora's box of security risks. If you think traditional IT security was tough, just wait until you see what happens when a cyberattack shuts down an entire production line or hijacks a SCADA system controlling a power grid. Spoiler alert: it's not pretty.

What is IIoT, and Why Should You Care?

At its core, Industrial IoT (IIoT) is about connecting industrial machines, sensors, and control systems to networks—often the internet. This connectivity allows for real-time data collection, remote monitoring, and predictive maintenance, making factories smarter and more efficient.

Think of IIoT as the big brother of consumer IoT (you know, smart thermostats, fridges that order milk when you're out, and doorbells that judge your Amazon addiction). But instead of controlling household devices, IIoT manages entire production lines, power grids, oil refineries, and water treatment plants. The stakes? A lot higher. If someone hacks your smart fridge, you might end up with spoiled milk. If someone hacks an IIoT-controlled chemical plant, we're talking about explosions, environmental disasters, and some very angry lawyers.

The main goal of IIoT is to improve efficiency, reduce costs, and increase automation. But here's the catch: the more connected things become, the more vulnerable they are to cyber threats. And guess what? Most industrial networks were never designed to be connected in the first place.

Inside the Smart Factory: The Good, the Bad, and the Hackable

A smart factory is essentially a traditional factory that's been injected with technology steroids. It's built on automation, robotics, AI-driven analytics, and IIoT devices that continuously exchange data. But let's break down what actually makes a factory "smart":

1. Industrial Sensors & IoT Devices

These little gadgets collect real-time data on everything—temperature, humidity, vibration, energy consumption, you name it. The problem? Most of them weren't built with security in mind. Hackers love exploiting unpatched sensors with weak authentication to get a foothold in industrial networks.

2. Programmable Logic Controllers (PLCs) and Industrial Control Systems (ICS)

PLCs are the brains behind factory automation. They control machines, production lines, and critical processes. The problem? Many PLCs were designed decades ago and still run on outdated protocols with zero encryption. If an attacker hijacks a PLC, they can manipulate production, sabotage machinery, or even shut down entire operations.

3. SCADA Systems (Supervisory Control and Data Acquisition)

SCADA is the command center of industrial networks. It allows operators to monitor and control large-scale industrial processes remotely. The issue? SCADA systems were originally designed for closed networks and never meant to be exposed to the internet. Today, many SCADA environments are accessible via the web, poorly secured, and prime targets for cyberattacks.

4. Cloud-Based IIoT Platforms & Data Analytics

Smart factories leverage cloud services to store and analyze massive amounts of operational data. AI-driven analytics help predict equipment failures before they happen and optimize production. But let's not ignore the elephant in the room—the cloud is a juicy target for attackers. A single misconfigured cloud instance can leak industrial secrets or allow attackers to manipulate critical operations.

5. Industrial Robotics and Automated Machinery

These robots don't just assemble cars and package products—they talk to each other, exchange data, and self-adjust to optimize performance. However, attackers have demonstrated that industrial robots can be remotely hijacked, allowing them to sabotage production, cause malfunctions, or even injure human workers. If that doesn't sound like a sci-fi horror story, I don't know what does.

IIoT Connectivity: The Double-Edged Sword

The good news? IIoT connectivity boosts efficiency, reduces downtime, and saves industries billions. The bad news? Every device that connects to a network expands the attack surface.

Many legacy industrial systems were designed with "security through obscurity"—meaning they were safe only because no one thought to hack them. Now that these systems are being plugged into the internet, attackers are having a field day scanning for exposed ICS devices using tools like Shodan and Censys.

It's like leaving your front door wide open with a giant neon sign saying "Valuables Inside"—except instead of stealing your TV, hackers could remotely manipulate factory machinery or disrupt national infrastructure.

So, What's the Fix?

Securing IIoT and smart factory environments isn't impossible—it just requires rethinking how we approach industrial cybersecurity. Here are some fundamental steps:

✓ **Network Segmentation** – Keep IIoT systems isolated from traditional IT networks. No direct internet exposure!

✓ **Zero Trust Security Model** – Assume nothing and no one inside your network is safe. Verify everything.

✓ **Regular Patching & Updates** – Many ICS/SCADA devices run on outdated firmware. Keep them patched or risk getting owned.

✓ **Strong Authentication** – Ditch default credentials and weak passwords (yes, "admin/admin" is still shockingly common).

✓ **Intrusion Detection & Monitoring** – Deploy anomaly detection systems to spot unusual activity before it turns into a full-blown attack.

✓ **Secure Industrial Protocols** – Implement encrypted communication and authentication mechanisms for ICS protocols like Modbus, DNP3, and OPC-UA.

Final Thoughts: Your Smart Factory is Only as Secure as Its Weakest Sensor

Look, IIoT is here to stay, and smart factories aren't going anywhere. They're faster, more efficient, and more intelligent than ever before. But intelligence without security is a disaster waiting to happen. The challenge isn't just keeping up with technology—it's making sure that technology doesn't become a hacker's playground.

So, next time you walk through a smart factory, just remember: every sensor, robot, and industrial control system is a potential entry point for attackers. Stay paranoid, stay secure, and never assume your factory is too boring to be hacked. Because trust me— hackers love an easy target.

1.2 Differences Between IT and OT Security in Industrial Environments

IT vs. OT: The Cybersecurity Cage Match Nobody Talks About

Picture this: A group of IT security professionals walks into a factory, looking smug and confident, armed with their firewalls, endpoint detection tools, and zero-trust policies. On the other side, a group of grizzled Operational Technology (OT) engineers, who have been running industrial control systems since Windows XP was cutting-edge, stare back with arms crossed. The IT team suggests regular software updates and network segmentation, and the OT team bursts into laughter. "You want us to reboot this machine? That would shut down production for six hours! Are you insane?"

Welcome to the never-ending battle between IT and OT security—two worlds that were never meant to mix, but now must work together in the age of Industrial IoT (IIoT). IT security is all about data protection, access controls, and confidentiality. OT security? It's about keeping the lights on, ensuring machines don't explode, and making sure a hacker can't turn a manufacturing plant into a scrapyard. Same end goal—completely different priorities.

What's the Big Difference?

At its core, the difference between Information Technology (IT) security and Operational Technology (OT) security comes down to what they protect and how they operate.

Aspect	IT Security	OT Security
Primary Goal	Protecting **data and information**	Ensuring **continuous operations and safety**
Key Concern	**Confidentiality** (keeping data private)	**Availability & Integrity** (keeping systems running safely)
Downtime Tolerance	Can handle short downtime for updates	Downtime = **huge financial losses, or worse, safety hazards**
Patching & Updates	Regular updates, frequent security patches	Patching is rare—**some systems run 15+ years on old firmware**
Network Design	Modern, internet-facing, cloud-integrated	Legacy, air-gapped (or at least should be)
Security Tools	Firewalls, SIEM, EDR, IDS/IPS, MFA	Physical controls, network segmentation, anomaly detection
Threat Impact	Data breaches, ransomware, phishing attacks	Catastrophic physical damage, safety risks, production shutdowns

Essentially, IT security protects data, OT security protects lives and machines. If an IT system gets hacked, the worst-case scenario might be a data leak or a ransom demand.

If an OT system gets hacked, the worst-case scenario could be a power plant meltdown, a gas pipeline explosion, or an entire city going dark.

The IT Security Mindset: Keep Data Safe at All Costs

In traditional IT security, the number one concern is confidentiality. Companies worry about data breaches, ransomware, phishing attacks, and insider threats. The standard IT security measures include:

- **Firewalls and Intrusion Detection Systems (IDS/IPS)** – Blocking unauthorized access and monitoring suspicious network activity.
- **Endpoint Detection and Response (EDR)** – Protecting employee devices from malware and exploits.
- **Regular Software Patching** – Ensuring operating systems and applications are up to date to prevent vulnerabilities.
- **Zero Trust Security Models** – Verifying every user, every device, every time to prevent unauthorized access.
- **Data Encryption and Backup Strategies** – Protecting sensitive information from leaks and ensuring recovery in case of cyberattacks.

IT teams prioritize cybersecurity hygiene—regular updates, password policies, and access restrictions. They assume that downtime is acceptable if it means improving security. But try telling an OT engineer that "we just need to reboot this PLC for an update", and you'll probably get escorted out of the building.

The OT Security Reality: Uptime is King

Operational Technology security is a different beast entirely. In industrial environments, availability and reliability matter more than anything else. Factories, power plants, and water treatment facilities CANNOT afford downtime.

OT systems often use legacy technology, like decades-old PLCs and SCADA systems, that were designed before cybersecurity was even a concern. Many of these systems:

✓ Run on outdated software and unpatched vulnerabilities

✓ Use hardcoded passwords that nobody dares to change

✓ Have zero encryption on communication protocols

✓ Were originally designed for air-gapped networks (but are now connected to IIoT systems anyway)

Updating or rebooting an OT system is not as simple as installing a Windows update. Some industrial machines must run 24/7 for years without interruption. If a system needs to be rebooted, it often requires meticulous planning, scheduled maintenance windows, and even physical safety checks to ensure nothing goes wrong.

Security measures in OT environments tend to focus on physical security, access controls, and anomaly detection rather than aggressive patching. Some key OT security strategies include:

- **Network Segmentation** – Keeping OT networks isolated from IT and internet-facing networks to reduce attack surfaces.
- **Strict Access Controls** – Only trusted operators should have access to critical control systems. No open remote desktop logins!
- **Anomaly Detection & Behavioral Monitoring** – Since traditional antivirus solutions don't work well in OT, many companies use AI-driven anomaly detection to spot unusual activity in industrial networks.
- **Defense-in-Depth** – Layering multiple security measures, including firewalls, intrusion prevention, and physical security controls.
- **Incident Response Plans** – Having backup procedures and failover systems in place if something goes wrong.

Bridging the IT-OT Security Gap

The problem is, IT and OT teams don't always see eye to eye. IT teams often push security updates and cloud-based solutions that make sense in an enterprise environment—but in an OT setting, those same updates could cause critical failures or introduce risks to physical safety.

To improve IIoT security, organizations need to bridge the IT-OT divide by:

✓ **Creating cross-disciplinary security teams** – IT and OT must work together instead of operating in silos.

✓ **Understanding each other's priorities** – IT teams need to respect OT's zero-downtime philosophy, and OT teams need to recognize that ignoring security entirely is not an option.

✓ **Implementing secure-by-design IIoT solutions** – Industrial networks should be built with security in mind from the start, not as an afterthought.

✓ **Using security solutions tailored for OT** – Instead of traditional endpoint antivirus software, use network-based anomaly detection that won't disrupt critical systems.

Final Thoughts: The IT vs. OT Rivalry is Over—Hackers Don't Care Which Side You're On

The truth is, attackers don't care whether a vulnerability exists in an IT or OT system—they'll exploit whatever they can. The NotPetya malware attack in 2017 crippled major industrial companies worldwide, causing billions in damage because IT systems were compromised, which then cascaded into OT environments.

It's time to stop treating IT and OT security as separate worlds. Modern smart factories, IIoT deployments, and connected infrastructure require a unified cybersecurity approach that protects both data and industrial processes.

So, IT pros—next time you walk into a factory, remember: a production shutdown is worse than a data breach in this world. And OT engineers—cyberattacks aren't just an IT problem anymore. Hackers don't care about your uptime concerns—but they'll happily take advantage of outdated firmware, weak passwords, and internet-exposed PLCs.

The future of cybersecurity is IT and OT working together—because hackers sure aren't waiting for us to figure it out.

1.3 Attack Surfaces in IIoT and SCADA Systems

Welcome to the Industrial Cybersecurity Horror Show

Imagine walking into a smart factory late at night. Machines hum, conveyor belts move, and robotic arms swing with perfect precision. Everything looks automated, efficient, and straight out of a sci-fi movie. But here's the twist—what if someone, sitting miles away in a dimly lit basement, hijacks the system and turns the factory against itself? Conveyor belts speed up, robotic arms go haywire, temperature sensors fail, and—before you know it—millions of dollars in production losses (or worse, a serious accident) unfold in real-time.

Welcome to the attack surface of Industrial IoT (IIoT) and SCADA systems, where cyber threats meet physical chaos. In IT environments, an attack usually means stolen data or financial losses. In industrial environments, an attack could mean explosions, environmental disasters, or even loss of human life. The stakes? Sky-high.

What is an Attack Surface?

An attack surface refers to all possible entry points a hacker can exploit to gain unauthorized access to a system. In an IIoT or SCADA environment, this includes:

Network infrastructure – Routers, firewalls, and poorly secured remote access points.

IIoT devices and sensors – Smart machines, temperature sensors, cameras, and industrial controllers.

SCADA & ICS software – Outdated, unpatched, or misconfigured applications.

Human operators – Phishing, weak passwords, and insider threats.

Supply chain vulnerabilities – Compromised hardware or software introduced by third-party vendors.

Unlike traditional IT systems, SCADA and IIoT networks were never designed with security in mind. Many legacy industrial control systems (ICS) still operate on 20-year-old firmware with default passwords like "admin123" that nobody ever bothered to change. Add the fact that more IIoT devices are being connected to the cloud, and you've got a massive attack surface just waiting to be exploited.

Major Attack Surfaces in IIoT and SCADA Systems

1. Unsecured IIoT Devices (The Dumb Smart Devices)

Industrial IoT devices are great—they provide real-time monitoring, automation, and efficiency. But here's the problem: most IIoT devices were built for functionality, not security.

Many IIoT sensors and controllers lack basic encryption and transmit data in plaintext.

Devices often come with hardcoded credentials (which hackers love to exploit).

Some IIoT devices can't be patched or updated, meaning any discovered vulnerability is a permanent security risk.

● **Attack Example**: In 2020, attackers exploited unsecured industrial IoT sensors in a water treatment plant, causing the system to manipulate water levels and chemical dosages. A tiny vulnerability in an IoT sensor nearly led to a public health disaster.

✓ **Defensive Strategy**: Change default passwords, enable encryption, and segment IIoT devices from critical control systems.

2. SCADA and ICS Protocol Vulnerabilities (The Open Doors Hackers Love)

SCADA systems use legacy communication protocols like Modbus, DNP3, and IEC 61850, which were designed decades ago—long before cybersecurity was a thing. Many of these protocols lack authentication and encryption, making them prime targets for Man-in-the-Middle (MITM) and injection attacks.

Modbus: Used in industrial automation but sends data in plaintext. Attackers can intercept and modify control commands.

DNP3: Common in power grids, but if not configured securely, attackers can send unauthorized control commands.

OPC-UA & MQTT: Modern IIoT protocols, but if misconfigured, they can be exploited for data exfiltration and system hijacking.

● **Attack Example**: The infamous Stuxnet worm (2010) manipulated SCADA protocols to sabotage Iranian nuclear centrifuges, proving that cyber-physical attacks are very real.

✓ **Defensive Strategy**: Use encrypted ICS protocols (TLS-secured OPC-UA), implement network segmentation, and deploy intrusion detection for abnormal SCADA commands.

3. Remote Access and VPN Exploits (When Convenience Turns into a Nightmare)

In the age of remote work, industrial engineers often access SCADA and ICS systems remotely using VPNs and Remote Desktop Protocol (RDP). But if these remote access points aren't properly secured, they become the easiest way for attackers to infiltrate industrial networks.

Many VPN credentials are weak or leaked on the dark web.

RDP servers are often publicly exposed, allowing brute-force attacks.

Attackers use stolen credentials to move laterally inside the OT network.

● **Attack Example**: In 2021, hackers exploited an exposed RDP server to gain access to a water treatment facility in Florida, attempting to increase the level of sodium hydroxide (lye) in drinking water to dangerous levels.

✓ **Defensive Strategy**: Use multi-factor authentication (MFA), enforce strong VPN policies, and deploy intrusion detection systems (IDS) to monitor remote access activity.

4. Supply Chain Attacks (When Your Own Vendors Become the Threat)

Even if your factory is secure, your vendors might not be. Attackers often target weak links in the supply chain to introduce compromised software updates, malicious firmware, or backdoored hardware into industrial environments.

● **Attack Example**: The SolarWinds attack (2020) was a classic supply chain compromise, where attackers inserted malware into legitimate software updates, affecting thousands of organizations, including critical infrastructure.

✓ **Defensive Strategy**: Vet your vendors, use hardware authentication, and deploy runtime security monitoring for supply chain risks.

5. Insider Threats (The Enemy Within)

Sometimes, the biggest security risks aren't hackers—they're employees. Whether it's a disgruntled worker sabotaging operations or an unaware engineer falling for a phishing email, insider threats remain one of the hardest risks to mitigate.

● **Attack Example**: In 2019, a disgruntled ex-employee of a wind turbine company used his old credentials to remotely disable turbines, causing widespread outages.

✓ **Defensive Strategy**: Revoke access for former employees immediately, monitor user activity, and use behavioral analytics to detect anomalies.

Final Thoughts: Attackers Don't Need to Blow Up a Factory—They Just Need One Weak Link

The reality of IIoT and SCADA security is that you're only as strong as your weakest link. Attackers don't need a sophisticated zero-day exploit—they just need one outdated sensor, one exposed VPN, or one forgotten default password to bring an entire system down.

Think of industrial cybersecurity like a medieval castle. You can have the tallest walls and strongest gates, but if someone leaves the side door open, the enemy walks right in.

So, are you going to be the cyber warrior who locks down your IIoT defenses—or are you going to let a forgotten factory sensor from 2005 be your downfall? The choice is yours.

1.4 Common Threats: Ransomware, Insider Attacks, and Cyber-Physical Risks

Welcome to the Industrial Cybersecurity Circus

Picture this: It's Monday morning. You stroll into the factory, coffee in one hand, a checklist in the other, ready to start the week. But instead of the usual hum of machines and glowing control screens, you see one giant ransom note plastered across every monitor:

"Your files have been encrypted. Pay 50 Bitcoin, or we turn your factory into a very expensive paperweight."

Meanwhile, your IT team is frantically trying to decrypt data, operators are locked out of control systems, and your CEO is on the verge of a heart attack because production losses are burning through cash faster than a hacker spends stolen crypto.

Congratulations, you've been hit by ransomware.

Welcome to the chaotic world of industrial cyber threats, where hackers, disgruntled employees, and even malfunctioning robots are all potential enemies. This chapter dives into the biggest threats facing Industrial IoT (IIoT) and SCADA systems today, including ransomware, insider attacks, and cyber-physical risks.

Let's break it down before the hackers do it for you.

1. Ransomware: Holding Factories Hostage

Ransomware is the bank robbery of the digital age. Instead of storming in with masks and guns, attackers encrypt your data and demand payment for the decryption key. Industrial environments are prime targets because:

Factories can't afford downtime – Every minute of lost production costs thousands (or millions) of dollars.

Legacy systems are easy targets – Many factories run outdated Windows XP or unpatched industrial software.

OT networks are often unprepared – Unlike IT environments, operational technology (OT) systems lack modern security protections like endpoint detection or behavioral analysis.

● **Attack Example**: In 2021, a ransomware attack shut down the Colonial Pipeline, causing fuel shortages across the U.S. The company ended up paying $4.4 million in Bitcoin to recover its systems.

✓ **Defensive Strategy**: Regularly back up critical data, segment IT and OT networks, implement multi-factor authentication (MFA), and train employees to avoid phishing scams.

2. Insider Threats: When the Call Comes from Inside the Factory

Not all threats come from hooded hackers in distant countries. Sometimes, the biggest danger is sitting inside your own factory, logging in with their employee credentials.

Insider threats come in two flavors:

Malicious insiders – Employees or contractors who intentionally sabotage systems, steal data, or sell access to hackers.

Negligent insiders – People who accidentally expose systems through weak passwords, clicking phishing emails, or misconfiguring security settings.

● **Attack Example**: In 2019, a disgruntled ex-employee of an energy company used his old credentials to remotely shut down wind turbines, causing massive power outages.

✅ **Defensive Strategy:** Use strict access control policies, monitor employee behavior with insider threat detection tools, and immediately revoke access for departing employees.

3. Cyber-Physical Risks: When Hacking Turns Dangerous

In IT environments, a successful cyber attack might mean stolen data. In industrial environments, a cyber attack can lead to physical destruction, explosions, or even loss of life.

Cyber-physical risks occur when hackers manipulate IIoT devices, SCADA systems, or industrial processes to cause real-world damage.

Hackers can shut down cooling systems, causing machines to overheat and fail.

They can manipulate chemical dosing in water plants, making water toxic.

They can trigger emergency shutdowns at power plants, causing blackouts.

● **Attack Example**: The Stuxnet attack (2010) sabotaged Iran's nuclear centrifuges by manipulating SCADA control systems, physically damaging equipment without detection.

✅ Defensive Strategy: Implement strict network segmentation, deploy anomaly detection systems to monitor industrial processes, and create fail-safe mechanisms to prevent unauthorized changes.

Final Thoughts: Don't Be the Next Cyber Victim

Hackers don't care if you're running a smart factory, power grid, or water treatment plant—if there's money to be made or chaos to be caused, they'll find a way in. Ransomware can hold your data hostage, insiders can betray your trust, and cyber-physical attacks can turn machines into weapons.

So, what's your plan? Will you wait for the inevitable cyber disaster, or will you take action today to lock down your IIoT and SCADA systems?

If you chose the second option, congratulations—you're already smarter than half the companies out there.

1.5 Regulatory and Compliance Standards (NIST, IEC 62443, NERC CIP)

Welcome to the World of Rules, Regulations, and Headaches

Ah, compliance—the word that strikes fear into engineers, makes auditors feel powerful, and forces cybersecurity teams to read painfully long PDFs. If you're working in Industrial IoT (IIoT) or SCADA security, you already know that regulations are as thrilling as watching paint dry, yet as critical as keeping oxygen in a space station.

But let's be real—nobody reads compliance documents for fun (except maybe auditors, and even that's debatable). They're long, confusing, and filled with enough legal jargon to make even a seasoned hacker want to switch careers. However, ignoring them is not an option.

Why? Because regulatory compliance isn't just about avoiding fines—it's about preventing disasters. Whether you're securing a power grid, a smart factory, or a water treatment plant, standards like NIST, IEC 62443, and NERC CIP exist to keep hackers from turning your industrial systems into chaos generators.

So, let's break these down without putting you to sleep.

Why Do These Standards Matter?

Unlike IT networks, where a breach might mean stolen data, an attack on industrial systems could mean:

Explosions at chemical plants

Blackouts affecting millions of people

Compromised water supplies

Billions in financial losses

Governments and industry groups developed cybersecurity frameworks to prevent these worst-case scenarios. Following these standards isn't just about compliance—it's about survival.

The Big Three: NIST, IEC 62443, and NERC CIP

1. NIST Cybersecurity Framework (The Swiss Army Knife of Security)

The National Institute of Standards and Technology (NIST) created the NIST Cybersecurity Framework (CSF) as a general guide for securing critical infrastructure. It provides a flexible, high-level approach to cybersecurity, meaning it's useful for both IT and OT environments.

The NIST framework is built on five core functions:

Identify – Understand what assets, systems, and risks you have.

Protect – Implement safeguards to prevent cyber attacks.

Detect – Continuously monitor for cyber threats.

Respond – Develop incident response plans.

Recover – Ensure systems can bounce back after an attack.

● **Why It Matters for IIoT:** NIST provides a broad, adaptable framework that works well for both traditional IT and industrial environments. If you're just getting started with security, this is the gold standard.

✓ **Key Takeaway**: If you don't know where to start, start with NIST.

2. IEC 62443 (The Industrial Cybersecurity Playbook)

While NIST is a broad framework, IEC 62443 is laser-focused on industrial control systems (ICS) and IIoT security. Developed by the International Electrotechnical Commission (IEC), this standard provides a detailed roadmap for securing industrial networks, devices, and applications.

IEC 62443 is broken down into four key areas:

General (IEC 62443-1-X) – Definitions, risk management, and foundational concepts.

Policies & Procedures (IEC 62443-2-X) – How organizations should manage cybersecurity at an operational level.

System Security (IEC 62443-3-X) – How to secure the overall industrial system and network.

Component Security (IEC 62443-4-X) – Security guidelines for IIoT devices, PLCs, and industrial hardware.

● **Why It Matters for IIoT**: IEC 62443 is designed specifically for industrial environments, making it one of the most relevant standards for smart factories and SCADA security.

✓ **Key Takeaway**: If your job involves securing OT systems, IEC 62443 is your best friend (or worst enemy, depending on how much you enjoy paperwork).

3. NERC CIP (The "No Blackouts Allowed" Rulebook)

The North American Electric Reliability Corporation (NERC) developed the Critical Infrastructure Protection (CIP) standards to secure power grids and energy infrastructure. If your company is involved in electricity generation, transmission, or distribution, you are legally required to follow NERC CIP.

NERC CIP focuses on:

Securing critical cyber assets (SCADA systems, energy management systems, etc.)

Implementing strict access controls

Incident response and recovery

Regular security audits and compliance reporting

● **Why It Matters for IIoT**: If you work in the energy sector, ignoring NERC CIP can result in multi-million-dollar fines and potential blackouts.

✓ **Key Takeaway**: If your company controls power plants or electrical grids, NERC CIP compliance isn't optional—it's the law.

Other Important Standards Worth Mentioning

ISO 27001 – A global information security standard, often used alongside NIST.

GDPR & CCPA – If your IIoT systems process personal data, privacy laws like GDPR (Europe) and CCPA (California) apply.

HIPAA – If you're working in medical IoT or smart healthcare, compliance with health data protection laws is mandatory.

The Harsh Truth: Compliance Doesn't Equal Security

Just because a company checks all the compliance boxes doesn't mean it's actually secure.

Regulations are often outdated – Cyber threats evolve faster than regulations can keep up.

Many companies treat compliance as a checkbox exercise – "We passed the audit, we're safe!" (Spoiler: You're not.)

Attackers don't care if you're compliant – They care about whether you left the digital backdoor open.

● **Real-World Example**: In 2015, hackers used stolen credentials and remote access tools to take down parts of Ukraine's power grid. The affected company was technically compliant with security standards—but compliance didn't stop the attack.

✓ **Key Lesson**: Compliance is the minimum standard, not the ultimate goal. Real security comes from continuous monitoring, adapting to new threats, and assuming you're already being targeted.

Final Thoughts: Compliance Isn't Fun, But It's Necessary

Look, I get it—nobody wakes up excited to read regulatory documents or pass security audits. But if you're securing IIoT, SCADA, or industrial control systems, compliance standards aren't just red tape—they're the blueprints for protecting critical infrastructure.

So, whether you're dealing with NIST, IEC 62443, or NERC CIP, here's my advice:

Don't just aim for compliance—aim for real security.

Use these frameworks as a starting point, not the finish line.

Hackers don't follow the rules—so neither should your security strategy.

At the end of the day, your job isn't just to pass an audit—it's to keep the factory running, the lights on, and the hackers out. 🚀

Chapter 2: Industrial Control System (ICS) and SCADA Security Fundamentals

Ah, SCADA systems—those mysterious, aging control networks that keep the world running while simultaneously making security experts lose sleep. If you think your home Wi-Fi is a pain to secure, imagine trying to protect an entire power grid with a system that predates the invention of the USB drive. That's the challenge of Industrial Control Systems (ICS)—they're the unsung heroes of manufacturing, energy, and infrastructure, yet they're riddled with hardcoded passwords, legacy software, and enough security holes to make Swiss cheese jealous.

This chapter provides an in-depth look at SCADA (Supervisory Control and Data Acquisition), Distributed Control Systems (DCS), and Programmable Logic Controllers (PLCs)—the backbone of industrial automation. We'll examine key ICS communication protocols, such as Modbus, DNP3, IEC 61850, and OPC-UA, as well as common vulnerabilities in legacy ICS systems. Additionally, we'll explore modern security strategies, including edge computing and AI-driven threat detection, to mitigate cyber risks in industrial environments.

2.1 Overview of SCADA, DCS, and PLC-Based Systems

Welcome to the Control System Zoo!

If you've ever walked into an industrial control room, you know it looks like something straight out of a sci-fi movie—massive screens flashing data, blinking lights on control panels, and engineers pressing buttons with the intensity of NASA mission control. But underneath all the cool tech is a complex web of systems that keep industries running 24/7.

Enter the three musketeers of industrial automation: SCADA, DCS, and PLCs. These systems don't just control machinery; they run entire cities, power grids, factories, water treatment plants, and even roller coasters.

Now, if you've ever wondered why factories don't just use regular computers to control industrial processes, here's the simple answer: because you don't want Windows Update rebooting your nuclear power plant mid-operation.

Industrial control systems (ICS) are designed for stability, reliability, and real-time operation—they prioritize keeping machines running over getting the latest security patch. This, of course, is both a feature and a security nightmare (but we'll get to that in later chapters).

For now, let's break down SCADA, DCS, and PLCs, so you know who does what in the industrial automation world.

1. SCADA (Supervisory Control and Data Acquisition) – The Big Boss

Imagine SCADA as the overlord of industrial automation. It doesn't directly control machines but watches over everything like a digital god, collecting data, analyzing trends, and sending commands to lower-level control systems.

What SCADA Does:

Monitors industrial processes in real-time (think water flow in a dam, pressure levels in oil pipelines, or voltage in power grids).

Collects and logs data for performance analysis and regulatory compliance.

Provides remote control capabilities—an operator in New York can shut down a pump in Texas.

Generates alerts and alarms when things go south (before they explode).

Where SCADA is Used:

SCADA is found in:

✓ Power grids (monitoring voltage, power loads, and outages)

✓ Water treatment plants (managing pumps, chemical dosing, and filtration)

✓ Oil and gas pipelines (detecting leaks, managing flow rates)

✓ Manufacturing plants (tracking production, controlling automated lines)

SCADA in Action:

Think of SCADA as a traffic control center for an entire city. It doesn't control every traffic light directly but analyzes data from sensors, adjusts signals, and makes sure there's no carmageddon.

● **Security Risk**: Because SCADA connects to remote industrial sites, it's a prime target for cyberattacks. Hackers love breaking into SCADA systems because shutting down a power grid from a laptop halfway across the world is their idea of a good time.

✓ **Key Takeaway**: SCADA is the brain of industrial automation—it doesn't operate machines directly but supervises everything.

2. DCS (Distributed Control System) – The Factory Foreman

If SCADA is the big boss, DCS is the hardworking middle manager who oversees production at the local level.

What DCS Does:

Controls complex industrial processes in real-time (like refining oil or producing pharmaceuticals).

Automates entire sections of a factory by coordinating multiple control loops.

Ensures process stability—if temperature or pressure goes out of range, DCS adjusts it automatically.

Provides redundancy—if one controller fails, another takes over to prevent downtime.

Where DCS is Used:

✓ **Refineries** (controlling temperature, pressure, and chemical reactions)
✓ **Chemical plants** (managing mixing, heating, and cooling)
✓ **Power plants** (optimizing turbine performance and fuel flow)
✓ **Pharmaceutical production** (ensuring drug manufacturing consistency)

DCS in Action:

Imagine you're brewing beer at an industrial scale. A DCS will control the temperature, manage the fermentation process, and adjust ingredient flows, ensuring that every bottle tastes exactly the same (and doesn't explode from too much pressure).

● **Security Risk**: While DCS networks are typically isolated, newer systems integrate with corporate IT networks, increasing their exposure to cyber threats.

✓ **Key Takeaway**: DCS automates and stabilizes industrial processes, ensuring consistency and efficiency.

3. PLCs (Programmable Logic Controllers) – The Workhorse

PLCs are the foot soldiers of industrial automation. If SCADA is the general and DCS is the captain, PLCs are the boots-on-the-ground workers who actually push the buttons and pull the levers.

What PLCs Do:

Control individual machines and processes (turning pumps on/off, opening valves, running conveyor belts).

Execute simple logic-based decisions (IF temperature > 100°C, THEN open valve).

Operate in harsh environments (factories, oil rigs, wastewater plants).

Run 24/7 without crashing (unlike your office laptop).

Where PLCs are Used:

✓ **Manufacturing lines** (automating assembly and packaging)
✓ **Robotic systems** (controlling industrial arms and welding machines)
✓ **Traffic lights** (managing green-red cycles)
✓ **Theme park rides** (ensuring roller coasters don't go flying off the tracks)

PLCs in Action:

Imagine you're running a bottling plant. A PLC controls:

✓ The conveyor belt speed

✓ The filling station (ensuring the right amount of liquid)

✓ The capping mechanism

✓ Rejecting defective bottles

It does all this with millisecond precision, ensuring everything flows like a well-oiled machine.

● **Security Risk**: Since PLCs were never designed with cybersecurity in mind, they're one of the weakest links in industrial security. Many still have hardcoded passwords from the 1990s.

✓ **Key Takeaway**: PLCs handle machine-level automation, making them essential for industrial operations.

Final Thoughts: Who's in Charge?

To sum it up:

SCADA is the big-picture supervisor that monitors and manages industrial processes remotely.

DCS is the process controller that keeps everything running smoothly on-site.

PLCs are the hands-on workers that directly control machines and devices.

If industrial automation were a military operation, it would look like this:

☐ **SCADA = The General** (Supervises the entire battlefield)
☐ **DCS = The Captain** (Manages local squads and operations)
☼ **PLCs = The Soldiers** (Do the actual fighting—aka controlling machines)

Each system plays a crucial role, and understanding how they interact is key to securing them against cyber threats. Because let's be honest—we don't want hackers taking over power plants, oil rigs, or roller coasters anytime soon. 🚀

2.2 ICS Communication Protocols: Modbus, DNP3, IEC 61850, OPC-UA

Talking Machines: The Secret Language of Industrial Systems

Ever wonder how giant industrial machines talk to each other? Well, it's not through WhatsApp or Zoom calls (though wouldn't that be funny? "Hey, Boiler-23, how's the pressure today?"). Instead, they communicate using Industrial Control System (ICS) protocols—specialized languages designed to keep factories, power plants, and water treatment facilities running smoothly.

The problem? Many of these protocols were designed decades ago—back when "security" meant locking the control room door and hoping for the best. These protocols were built for reliability and efficiency, not cybersecurity. Hackers love that. Why? Because intercepting and manipulating these communications is like hijacking an unencrypted walkie-talkie conversation—just too easy.

Let's break down the four major players in the ICS protocol world: Modbus, DNP3, IEC 61850, and OPC-UA.

1. Modbus: The Granddaddy of ICS Protocols

What It Is:

Modbus is one of the oldest and most widely used ICS communication protocols. Developed in 1979 by Modicon, it was originally meant for programmable logic controllers (PLCs) to talk to each other. And just like bell-bottom jeans, it's still around decades later, despite being horribly outdated.

Where It's Used:

✓ Power plants

✓ Water treatment facilities

✓ Manufacturing lines

✓ Oil and gas pipelines

How It Works:

Uses a simple master-slave architecture (one device gives orders, others obey).

Originally used serial connections (RS-232/RS-485) but has since moved to Modbus TCP/IP for networked environments.

No built-in security—data is sent in plain text with no authentication.

Security Nightmare:

Modbus is like an old radio station broadcasting factory commands in plain text. Anyone with network access can listen in, modify commands, or even shut down operations. That's why attackers love it—it's ridiculously easy to manipulate.

🔊 **Attack Example**: A hacker can spoof Modbus traffic and trick a power plant into shutting down generators, causing a blackout.

✅ **Fix It**: If you must use Modbus, wrap it in encryption tunnels (like TLS VPNs) and segment your network to keep unauthorized users out.

2. DNP3: The Utility Workhorse

What It Is:

Distributed Network Protocol 3 (DNP3) was developed in the 1990s to address the shortcomings of Modbus, particularly for electric utilities and water systems.

Where It's Used:

✅ Power grids

✅ Substations

✅ Water and wastewater plants

How It Works:

More advanced than Modbus, supports time-stamped data and event-driven messaging.

Can work over serial, Ethernet, or wireless networks.

Originally had no encryption or authentication, but newer versions support Secure DNP3 (which almost nobody implements).

Security Weakness:

DNP3 is better than Modbus but still hackable. Since many deployments still use unencrypted versions, attackers can spoof commands or replay previous messages to manipulate critical infrastructure.

⚖ **Attack Example**: Hackers can intercept DNP3 traffic and send a "shutdown" command to an entire electrical substation, taking out power to a city.

✅ **Fix It**: Use Secure DNP3, apply firewalls and deep packet inspection (DPI) to monitor traffic, and restrict access to critical networks.

3. IEC 61850: The Smart Grid Standard

What It Is:

IEC 61850 is a modern, Ethernet-based protocol designed for substation automation and smart grids. It replaces older protocols with faster, more flexible communication methods.

Where It's Used:

✅ Electrical substations

✅ Smart grids

✅ Power generation plants

How It Works:

Uses object-oriented data models (basically, instead of just raw data, devices exchange meaningful information).

Supports real-time communication and automation across substations.

Unlike Modbus and DNP3, it was built with networking in mind, using standard TCP/IP and Ethernet.

Security Weakness:

IEC 61850 wasn't designed with cybersecurity as a priority. Though it's more advanced than Modbus or DNP3, it relies on the underlying network for security—which isn't always properly configured.

Attack Example: If an attacker gains access to a substation network, they can spoof IEC 61850 messages, altering power flow and causing serious disruptions.

✅ **Fix It**: Implement network segmentation, strong authentication, and encrypted communication between substations.

4. OPC-UA: The Secure, Modern Standard (Kind of)

What It Is:

OPC Unified Architecture (OPC-UA) is a next-generation industrial protocol designed for secure, cross-platform communication between industrial devices and IT systems.

Where It's Used:

✅ Industrial automation (factories, manufacturing)

✅ Smart factories (Industry 4.0)

✅ IoT-enabled industrial environments

How It Works:

Uses object-oriented communication, meaning devices exchange structured data instead of just raw numbers.

Supports end-to-end encryption and authentication (finally, some security!).

Works across Windows, Linux, embedded systems, and cloud environments.

Security Strengths:

OPC-UA is the first ICS protocol built with security in mind—it includes encryption, authentication, and access control out of the box. But, here's the catch: many companies turn off security features because they find them "too complicated." ☐

Attack Example: If security settings are disabled, attackers can spoof OPC-UA messages and manipulate industrial processes.

☑ **Fix It**: Enable security features! Use TLS encryption, strong authentication, and proper access control to lock things down.

Final Thoughts: The Good, The Bad, and The Insecure

When it comes to ICS communication protocols, most were never designed with security in mind. Here's a quick recap:

Protocol	Strengths	Weaknesses
Modbus	Simple, widely used	No security, easy to hijack
DNP3	Better than Modbus, event-driven	Still lacks proper encryption
IEC 61850	Fast, great for smart grids	Network security depends on configuration
OPC-UA	Secure, modern, cross-platform	Security is often **disabled** by lazy admins 😒

What You Can Do:

Segregate ICS networks from IT networks (don't let random users access critical systems).

Enable encryption and authentication on protocols that support it.

Use firewalls and deep packet inspection to detect unauthorized protocol traffic.

Train your engineers and security teams—because a fancy security system is useless if people don't use it properly.

In short, ICS protocols are like old castles—built for strength but never designed for modern cyber warfare. It's up to us to reinforce the walls, install security cameras, and maybe, just maybe, stop hackers from storming the gates. 🏰🔒

2.3 Identifying Vulnerabilities in Legacy ICS and SCADA Systems

Legacy ICS and SCADA: The Ancient Relics Still Running the World

If you've ever seen an ancient mainframe running a critical power grid, you'd probably ask, "Wait... this thing is still working?" Yep. Welcome to the world of Legacy Industrial Control Systems (ICS) and SCADA (Supervisory Control and Data Acquisition) systems, where decades-old technology still runs factories, water plants, and even nuclear reactors.

Now, here's the fun part (or terrifying part, depending on your perspective): many of these systems were designed in the 80s and 90s, back when hackers were just kids messing around with floppy disks. Cybersecurity? What's that? These systems were built to last forever—and guess what? They did. But they were never built to withstand modern cyber threats.

The result? Massive security vulnerabilities that hackers can exploit with minimal effort. And let's be honest: when your industrial system is running on Windows XP and still has the default password set to 'admin', you've got bigger problems than just a lack of software updates.

So, what makes these legacy systems so vulnerable? Let's break it down.

1. Hardcoded Credentials: The Skeleton Keys for Attackers

Imagine locking your front door but leaving a spare key under the doormat. That's essentially what hardcoded credentials do for hackers.

Why It's a Problem:

Many legacy ICS and SCADA devices come with default usernames and passwords that were never meant to be changed.

Some vendors hardcoded credentials directly into firmware, meaning even if you wanted to change them, you couldn't.

Attackers can easily find these credentials in user manuals, online documentation, or by simply Googling "default SCADA passwords." (Seriously, try it.)

🔊 Real-World Example:

Attackers used default passwords on Siemens PLCs to gain unauthorized access to a water treatment facility, altering chemical levels in drinking water.

✅ **Fix It:**

Change default passwords immediately (assuming you actually can).

Use multi-factor authentication (MFA) for critical systems.

Replace devices that don't allow credential changes (if possible).

2. No Encryption = Open Invitations for Hackers

Would you send your banking information through an unsecured, public Wi-Fi network? Of course not. But that's exactly how legacy SCADA systems operate—all communication happens in plain text, making it incredibly easy for attackers to intercept and manipulate data.

Why It's a Problem:

Legacy SCADA systems use unencrypted protocols like Modbus, DNP3, and older versions of OPC.

Hackers can perform Man-in-the-Middle (MITM) attacks to intercept and modify commands.

Spoofed SCADA commands can cause real-world damage, such as opening floodgates or shutting down power grids.

🔒 **Real-World Example:**

In 2015, hackers intercepted unencrypted SCADA traffic in Ukraine's power grid attack, shutting down electricity for 230,000 people.

✅ **Fix It:**

Use VPNs and encrypted tunnels to protect SCADA communications.

Implement secure versions of ICS protocols (e.g., Secure DNP3, OPC-UA with encryption).

Monitor network traffic for suspicious activity.

3. Outdated Software: The Cybersecurity Time Bomb

Do you know what's scarier than a hacker? A Windows XP machine running a nuclear power plant. ☹

Why It's a Problem:

Many ICS and SCADA systems still run on outdated operating systems (Windows XP, Windows 2000, and even DOS).

No security patches means vulnerabilities remain exploitable forever.

Many legacy systems can't be updated because they are tightly integrated into industrial processes.

🔎 Real-World Example:

The WannaCry ransomware attack in 2017 crippled hospitals, manufacturing plants, and industrial systems because they were still running Windows XP—which Microsoft had stopped supporting years earlier.

✅ Fix It:

Patch and update whenever possible.

If updates aren't possible, isolate legacy systems from external networks.

Use application whitelisting to prevent unauthorized software from running.

4. Air Gaps: The Myth of Isolation

Many industrial operators believe in the "air gap" fairy tale—the idea that because their SCADA system isn't connected to the internet, it's automatically safe. That's wrong.

Why It's a Problem:

Many "air-gapped" systems are actually connected to the internet without operators realizing it.

Employees use USB drives to transfer data between secure and non-secure systems—and that's all it takes for malware to spread.

Attackers can use supply chain attacks to introduce malware before the system is even installed.

🔒 Real-World Example:

The Stuxnet worm (which destroyed Iran's nuclear centrifuges) spread through infected USB drives, bypassing the so-called "air gap."

✅ Fix It:

Physically restrict USB and removable media access.

Monitor network activity—even "air-gapped" networks can still be compromised.

Use Data Diodes (one-way communication devices) to truly isolate critical systems.

5. Lack of Security Monitoring: Attackers Love Blind Spots

You can't stop a hacker if you don't even know they're in your system. Unfortunately, most ICS and SCADA operators don't have real-time monitoring for security threats.

Why It's a Problem:

Many industrial environments only monitor for equipment failures, not cyber threats.

Attackers can stay undetected for months or years before launching an attack.

No logging or forensic capabilities means you can't even investigate after an attack happens.

🔒 Real-World Example:

The Triton malware attack on a Saudi petrochemical plant in 2017 remained undetected for months, giving attackers full control over safety systems.

✅ Fix It:

Deploy intrusion detection systems (IDS) for ICS networks.

Implement behavioral monitoring to detect anomalies.

Conduct regular security audits to find vulnerabilities before attackers do.

Final Thoughts: Legacy Systems Are a Hacker's Playground

Here's the brutal truth: most ICS and SCADA systems are ridiculously outdated and insecure—but they're still running critical infrastructure around the world.

Key Takeaways:

Hardcoded passwords, no encryption, and outdated software make legacy SCADA systems easy targets.

The air gap myth is dangerous—USB drives and insider threats can bypass isolation.

Attackers love the lack of security monitoring in industrial environments.

What You Can Do:

✅ Change default passwords and remove hardcoded credentials.

✅ Enable encryption wherever possible.

✅ Update and patch systems when feasible—or isolate them properly if you can't.

✅ Deploy intrusion detection to catch attacks before they cause damage.

At the end of the day, legacy ICS and SCADA security is about survival—either we secure these aging systems before hackers do, or we wait for the next massive industrial cyberattack to remind us why we should have acted sooner. 💀

2.4 The Role of Edge Computing and AI in Industrial Security

AI, Edge Computing, and Industrial Security: The Future is Now (And a Bit Terrifying)

Let's be honest—when most people hear "AI and industrial security", they either picture a sci-fi utopia where robots handle everything or a dystopian nightmare where Skynet takes over factories and launches an all-out cyber war. Reality, as always, sits somewhere in between.

The truth is, industrial environments are getting smarter, and with that intelligence comes both incredible opportunities and terrifying risks. On one hand, AI-powered security and edge computing can detect and prevent cyberattacks in real time, making industrial systems more resilient and efficient. On the other hand, hackers are already figuring out how to outsmart AI defenses, and a compromised AI could become the ultimate cyber weapon.

So, should we embrace AI and edge computing in industrial security? Absolutely. But we need to do it the right way, because if history has taught us anything, it's that every new technology brings both solutions and fresh ways to get hacked.

What is Edge Computing, and Why Does It Matter?

Before we dive into the AI-powered security cool stuff, let's talk about edge computing—because without it, industrial AI is like a superhero without powers.

The Problem: Centralized Cloud Processing is Too Slow for Industrial Security

Traditional industrial security solutions rely on centralized cloud computing. That means all security data from industrial devices (SCADA systems, PLCs, sensors, etc.) has to be sent to the cloud for analysis before any action is taken. Sounds fine in theory, but in reality:

Network latency: If an attack happens, waiting for a cloud-based security system to process data could mean the difference between preventing a breach and a full-scale disaster.

Bandwidth overload: Industrial environments generate massive amounts of data—sending everything to the cloud is inefficient and expensive.

Cyber risks: The more data you send over the network, the more attack surfaces you expose.

The Solution: Process Security Data Locally (at the Edge)

Edge computing moves security processing closer to the source of data. Instead of relying on cloud servers, security decisions can be made on-site, in real-time, using AI-powered edge devices.

✅ Faster threat detection

✅ Reduced network dependency

✅ More control over industrial security data

Think of it this way: instead of sending every security alert to a "boss" in the cloud, edge devices can make smart decisions on their own, like an experienced factory worker handling small problems without waiting for a manager's approval.

How AI is Revolutionizing Industrial Security

Alright, now let's talk about AI—the brain behind modern industrial security. Here's how artificial intelligence is changing the game.

1. AI-Powered Threat Detection (Goodbye, Signature-Based Antivirus)

Remember the good old days when antivirus software just looked for known malware signatures? Yeah, that doesn't work in industrial security anymore. Attackers are using zero-day exploits, polymorphic malware, and AI-generated attacks that traditional methods can't detect.

How AI Helps:

AI can analyze huge amounts of security data in real-time to spot anomalous behavior before an attack happens.

Behavior-based detection means AI can identify suspicious activity, even if the attack has never been seen before.

AI-powered security systems can automatically respond to threats, shutting down malicious activity without human intervention.

🔎 **Example**: An AI-powered system detects an unusual spike in PLC traffic, indicating a potential ransomware attack. Instead of waiting for a human to investigate, the AI isolates the affected device and prevents the spread of malware.

2. Predictive Maintenance: Stopping Attacks Before They Happen

Wouldn't it be great if your industrial security system could predict cyberattacks before they happen? That's exactly what AI-powered predictive analytics can do.

How AI Helps:

AI can monitor industrial equipment in real-time, spotting early warning signs of cyber threats.

Machine learning algorithms can identify patterns in attack attempts, helping companies harden vulnerable systems before hackers exploit them.

AI can prioritize security alerts, reducing false positives so security teams don't waste time chasing ghosts.

🏛 **Example**: AI detects unusual login attempts on SCADA workstations outside of normal operating hours. Instead of waiting for an attack, the system blocks access and alerts security teams instantly.

3. AI-Powered Incident Response (Because Humans Can't Respond Fast Enough)

Cyberattacks happen in milliseconds. Human security teams? Not so much.

How AI Helps:

AI-powered automated incident response systems can react instantly to security threats.

AI can shut down compromised devices, isolate infected networks, and even reverse engineer malware in real-time.

AI-driven forensic analysis helps security teams understand attack patterns and strengthen defenses.

🏛 **Example**: A SCADA network detects a brute-force login attack on a power plant's remote access system. Instead of waiting for IT to investigate, the AI system immediately blocks the attacker's IP address and forces all users to reauthenticate.

The Security Risks of AI and Edge Computing (Yes, Even AI Can Get Hacked)

Of course, nothing is invincible—and AI-powered security is no exception. Here's how attackers can exploit AI and edge computing:

1. AI Manipulation (Adversarial Attacks)

Hackers can trick AI security systems by feeding them malicious, misleading data—essentially making them blind to real threats.

2. Compromising Edge Devices

Since edge devices handle critical security processing, attackers target them to gain control over security defenses.

3. AI-Powered Attacks

Attackers are using AI, too—from AI-generated phishing scams to automated malware that learns how to evade detection.

Final Thoughts: AI and Edge Computing Are the Future (But Use Them Wisely)

There's no doubt that AI and edge computing are transforming industrial security—but like any powerful technology, they must be used wisely.

Key Takeaways:

✓ Edge computing reduces latency, improves security, and keeps industrial systems running smoothly.

✓ AI-powered security systems detect, prevent, and respond to threats faster than humans ever could.

✓ Hackers are also using AI—so AI-powered defenses must constantly evolve.

What You Can Do:

◆ Implement AI-driven threat detection in industrial environments.
◆ Deploy edge computing for real-time security processing.
◆ Stay ahead of attackers by continuously updating AI models.

At the end of the day, AI won't replace human security teams—but it will give them a fighting chance in a world where industrial cyber threats are more sophisticated than ever.

2.5 Hardening SCADA and ICS Systems Against Cyber Threats

Securing SCADA and ICS: Because Hackers Love Industrial Chaos

You ever wake up in a cold sweat, wondering if some hacker on the other side of the world is about to take control of a power plant, open a dam, or shut down a factory just for fun? No? Well, you should.

SCADA (Supervisory Control and Data Acquisition) and ICS (Industrial Control Systems) were designed for reliability and efficiency—not cybersecurity. A lot of these systems are older than your Wi-Fi router and about as secure as leaving your front door wide open with a neon sign that says, "Come on in!"

Hackers know this. That's why industrial systems have become some of the juiciest targets for cybercriminals, nation-state attackers, and ransomware gangs. The good news? We can fight back—but it's going to take a serious mindset shift and some solid security strategies to lock these systems down.

Why Are SCADA and ICS So Vulnerable?

Industrial control systems were never built for the internet. The idea that factories, power plants, and water treatment facilities would one day be connected to a global network wasn't even a consideration when many of these systems were designed.

Here's why SCADA and ICS are so easy to exploit:

Legacy Systems That Can't Be Patched – Some ICS environments are still running Windows XP (yes, really).

Flat Networks with No Segmentation – Attackers can move laterally from one device to another with no obstacles.

Default Credentials – Many industrial devices still use factory-set passwords, making them easy targets.

No Built-In Security – Traditional IT security solutions don't work well in ICS environments. Installing antivirus software on a PLC? Not happening.

Remote Access Without Proper Controls – Thanks to the rise of IIoT, many SCADA systems are now accessible from anywhere. That's great for convenience, but also great for hackers.

So, how do we fix this mess? Let's talk about hardening SCADA and ICS environments.

1. Network Segmentation: Stop the Lateral Movement

Imagine if every door in a factory was unlocked—a thief could walk right in and take whatever they wanted. That's how many ICS networks are set up. No segmentation means one compromised device = full system access.

✅ The Fix:

Separate IT and OT networks—don't let your office Wi-Fi connect to your industrial control network.

Use VLANs and firewalls to segment different systems and limit traffic.

Implement a DMZ between corporate and ICS networks to prevent direct access.

🔒 Real-World Example:

A hacker breached a casino's network through a smart fish tank thermometer (yes, really) and moved laterally to access high-value systems. Imagine what they could do in a factory.

2. Implement a Zero Trust Model: Trust No One

The old cybersecurity model was based on trusting devices inside the network. Guess what? That doesn't work anymore. Zero Trust assumes that no device, user, or network segment is safe.

✅ The Fix:

Verify every access request (even if it comes from inside the network).

Use multi-factor authentication (MFA) for all remote and privileged access.

Enforce the principle of least privilege—only give users and devices the access they absolutely need.

3. Secure Remote Access: Stop Letting Attackers Walk In

Many SCADA and ICS breaches happen because remote access is wide open—either through exposed RDP servers, weak VPNs, or default credentials that attackers can guess in minutes.

✅ The Fix:

Use VPNs with strong encryption—no more outdated PPTP VPNs.

Implement jump servers instead of direct remote access to critical systems.

Enable logging and monitoring for all remote connections.

📷 Real-World Example:

In 2021, hackers breached a Florida water treatment facility by remotely accessing a SCADA system and attempting to poison the water supply. If better remote access controls had been in place, the attack never would have happened.

4. Lock Down Industrial Devices: No More Default Passwords

If I had a dollar for every SCADA system still using default admin passwords, I'd be rich. Attackers scan the internet daily for exposed ICS devices with weak or factory-set credentials.

✅ The Fix:

Change all default passwords immediately.

Use strong, unique passwords for every system and device.

Disable unnecessary services and ports to reduce the attack surface.

🔊 Real-World Example:

A hacker gained access to a power plant by guessing the default password on an industrial router. One weak password = total system compromise.

5. Monitor and Detect Threats in Real Time

Most industrial environments have little to no visibility into cyber threats. If an attacker breaches a SCADA system, how would you even know?

✅ The Fix:

Deploy intrusion detection systems (IDS) for ICS networks.

Use anomaly detection—AI-powered tools can spot unusual behavior before an attack spreads.

Log and monitor all ICS traffic—you can't protect what you can't see.

6. Patch and Update (When Possible)

I know, I know—patching ICS devices is tricky because downtime is expensive. But leaving vulnerabilities unpatched is far more dangerous.

✅ The Fix:

Prioritize patching critical vulnerabilities—especially for devices with internet access.

Use virtual patching if applying traditional patches isn't possible.

Regularly audit and assess system vulnerabilities.

🔊 Real-World Example:

Stuxnet spread through unpatched Windows systems in an Iranian nuclear facility, causing massive damage. If proper patching and security controls had been in place, the attack would have failed.

Final Thoughts: Harden Your ICS Before Hackers Do It For You

Cybercriminals are getting smarter, faster, and more persistent—and they love attacking industrial environments.

If we don't take ICS security seriously, hackers will keep winning. But with the right strategies, we can fight back:

- 🔥 Segment your network
- 🔥 Implement Zero Trust
- 🔥 Secure remote access
- 🔥 Change default passwords
- 🔥 Monitor for threats
- 🔥 Patch and update when possible

At the end of the day, securing SCADA and ICS systems isn't just about cybersecurity— it's about keeping critical infrastructure running, protecting lives, and ensuring industrial operations don't fall into the hands of bad actors.

Because let's be real—the only people who should have control over your factory, power plant, or water facility are the ones actually working there—not some hacker sitting in their pajamas across the world. 🚀

Chapter 3: Network Security in Smart Factories

Imagine your factory floor as a digital jungle—data flying around like hyperactive monkeys, devices talking to each other in strange industrial dialects, and hackers lurking in the shadows, waiting for the perfect moment to strike. IIoT networks are a hacker's playground, often riddled with poorly segmented architectures, misconfigured devices, and network security policies that haven't been updated since dial-up was a thing. If your factory's firewall is the only thing standing between you and a cyberattack, you're in for a wild ride.

This chapter focuses on network security principles for smart factories, covering secure network architectures, segmentation strategies, and Zero Trust security models. We'll discuss common network vulnerabilities in IIoT environments, including exposed devices, weak authentication mechanisms, and the risks of flat networks. Additionally, we'll explore best practices for securing ICS and OT networks against MITM (Man-in-the-Middle) attacks, packet injection, and lateral movement by attackers.

3.1 Designing Secure Network Architectures for IIoT

Building Fort Knox for Industrial IoT (Without the Moat and Drawbridge)

Alright, let's get real for a second. If you think your factory's IIoT devices are safe just because they're behind a basic firewall, I've got some bad news—you might as well be locking your front door but leaving all the windows wide open. Industrial IoT security isn't just about protection—it's about smart design from the ground up.

IIoT networks are growing faster than your unread email count, and with that comes a massive attack surface. A poorly designed network means attackers can hop from one vulnerable device to another like a digital parkour course. If we want to keep hackers, malware, and cybercriminals out, we need to design IIoT networks like we're building Fort Knox—but, you know, without the moat and armed guards (probably).

Why Traditional IT Network Design Won't Work for IIoT

Before we dive into best practices, let's clear up one common misconception: you cannot secure an IIoT network the same way you secure an IT network.

Here's why:

IIoT Devices Are Different – Unlike traditional IT systems, IIoT devices aren't just computers; they include industrial controllers, sensors, and actuators, many of which were never built with security in mind.

Real-Time Operations Matter – In industrial environments, latency is a deal-breaker. You can't just throw every security tool at an IIoT network and hope for the best.

Downtime = Financial Disaster – Industrial networks can't afford frequent security updates or patches like traditional IT networks. A single minute of downtime can mean millions in losses.

Attack Surfaces Are Vast – IIoT introduces more wireless connections, remote access points, and cloud integrations, meaning there are far more entry points for hackers.

So, how do we design an IIoT network that's both secure and functional? Let's break it down.

Step 1: Implement Network Segmentation (Because Flat Networks Are a Hacker's Playground)

Many industrial environments still use flat networks, meaning every device—whether it's a PLC, an IoT sensor, or an engineer's laptop—is connected on the same network with no restrictions. This is an absolute nightmare from a security perspective.

✅ The Fix:

Use VLANs (Virtual LANs) to separate different types of traffic. Keep IIoT devices, IT systems, and critical controllers on different segments.

Create an Industrial Demilitarized Zone (IDMZ) between the IT and OT networks. This acts as a security buffer that filters and inspects traffic before it reaches critical systems.

Block unnecessary communication between network segments. Not every device needs to talk to every other device—limit communication to only what is essential.

🚨 Real-World Example:

A hacker breached a U.S. manufacturing plant's corporate IT network through a phishing attack. Because the IT and OT networks were not segmented, they were able to pivot into the industrial control systems, causing massive disruptions. A properly segmented network would have stopped them cold.

Step 2: Apply the Principle of Least Privilege (Because Not Every Device Needs Full Access)

In too many IIoT environments, devices have way more access than they should. The result? If a hacker gets in, they can move freely and take down critical infrastructure in no time.

✅ **The Fix:**

Use Role-Based Access Control (RBAC) – Every user, system, and device should only have the minimum access needed to do its job.

Implement Micro-Segmentation – Instead of just segmenting at the network level, go deeper and restrict access between individual devices.

Use Strong Authentication – IIoT devices should never rely on default credentials or weak passwords (seriously, stop using "admin123").

📷 **Real-World Example:**

A water treatment facility in the U.S. was attacked in 2021 because a SCADA system was accessible through an employee's weak remote access credentials. The hacker tried to increase chemical levels in the water but was caught just in time. If proper access controls had been in place, this attack never would have happened.

Step 3: Secure IIoT Communication (Because Eavesdropping Isn't Just for Spies)

IIoT devices constantly send and receive data—but in many networks, this communication is completely unprotected. That means attackers can easily intercept, alter, or manipulate critical industrial commands.

✅ **The Fix:**

Use Encrypted Protocols – Avoid unencrypted protocols like plain-text Modbus. Instead, use secure alternatives like TLS-based OPC-UA.

Disable Unused Protocols – Many industrial devices still support old, insecure protocols. If you're not using them, turn them off.

Monitor Network Traffic – Use deep packet inspection (DPI) to detect unusual activity or potential attacks on industrial communication.

🔎 Real-World Example:

The Stuxnet worm spread through unsecured industrial protocols to sabotage Iran's nuclear centrifuges. A properly encrypted and monitored network could have stopped its spread.

Step 4: Implement Network Monitoring & Threat Detection (Because Prevention Isn't Enough)

Even the best-designed networks can still be breached. That's why continuous monitoring is essential. The sooner you detect a threat, the less damage it can do.

✅ The Fix:

Deploy an Industrial Intrusion Detection System (IDS) – Tools like Nozomi Networks or Dragos can detect anomalous activity in ICS environments.

Enable Logging and Alerting – Every login attempt, data transfer, and network request should be logged and reviewed regularly.

Use AI-Powered Threat Detection – Machine learning can help identify patterns of attack that humans might miss.

🔎 Real-World Example:

In 2017, a European energy company detected a brute-force attack on its SCADA system using an IDS before any damage was done. Without network monitoring, the attack could have caused a massive blackout.

Final Thoughts: Your IIoT Network Needs More Than Just a Firewall

If you've made it this far, congrats—you now understand that IIoT network security is way more than just slapping a firewall in place and calling it a day. Hackers are evolving, attacks are getting more sophisticated, and industrial environments are more connected than ever.

- 🔒 Segment your network
- 🔒 Apply least privilege access
- 🔒 Secure communication channels
- 🔒 Monitor everything, detect early

At the end of the day, a well-designed IIoT network isn't just about cybersecurity—it's about keeping factories running, critical infrastructure safe, and industrial chaos in check. Because the last thing we need is some hacker in their basement shutting down an entire factory just for the lulz. 🚀

3.2 Implementing Segmentation and Zero Trust Security Models

Your Network Isn't a Buffet—So Stop Giving Everything Unlimited Access

If your IIoT network were a restaurant, would you let anyone walk into the kitchen, grab a chef's knife, and start messing with the food? Of course not. (At least, I hope not.) But in too many industrial environments, networks are wide open, letting devices, users, and even hackers roam free like it's some kind of all-you-can-access buffet.

That's where segmentation and Zero Trust security come in. Think of segmentation as putting walls in place—keeping the waitstaff, the cooks, and the guests in separate areas so no one accidentally (or maliciously) messes with the critical operations. And Zero Trust? That's your paranoid head chef, constantly verifying who's allowed in and never assuming anyone is trustworthy.

The old way of securing IIoT networks—where everything inside the perimeter was trusted—is dead. Attackers are getting smarter, ransomware loves jumping between devices, and one exposed sensor could be all it takes to bring down an entire factory. It's time to lock things down.

Segmentation: Because Flat Networks Are a Disaster Waiting to Happen

A flat network means everything is connected with no restrictions. One breach, and an attacker can move laterally across your entire system. That's why segmentation is critical—it limits damage and isolates critical systems.

✅ **Key Segmentation Strategies:**

Network Segmentation with VLANs

Separate IIoT devices from IT systems

Isolate critical controllers from non-essential traffic

Prevent low-security devices from accessing high-security areas

Micro-Segmentation

Restrict access between devices on the same segment

Use firewall rules to allow only necessary communication

Implement device-specific access controls

Creating an Industrial DMZ (IDMZ)

Acts as a buffer zone between IT and OT networks

Filters and inspects traffic before reaching critical systems

Prevents malware from spreading across environments

📷 **Real-World Example:**

A global manufacturing company suffered a ransomware attack on its corporate IT network. Because the IT and OT networks were not segmented, the ransomware spread to SCADA systems, halting production for days. Proper segmentation would have contained the attack.

Zero Trust: The "Guilty Until Proven Innocent" Approach

Zero Trust isn't about not trusting your employees—it's about not trusting devices, applications, or networks by default. Even if a system is inside your network, it should not automatically be trusted.

✅ Core Principles of Zero Trust Security:

Verify Every User and Device

Use multi-factor authentication (MFA) for all logins

Enforce least privilege access (only give people what they absolutely need)

Limit Access with Software-Defined Perimeters (SDP)

Only allow access to specific applications instead of full network access

Hide internal systems from external users unless explicitly authorized

Continuous Monitoring and Adaptive Authentication

Use AI-driven security tools to detect unusual behavior

If a system suddenly starts acting suspicious, re-authenticate it or cut it off

📷 Real-World Example:

A cybercriminal compromised a contractor's VPN login credentials and gained access to an oil refinery's internal network. Because the refinery relied on a traditional perimeter-based security model, the attacker was able to move laterally and access industrial control systems. With a Zero Trust model, the login would have been continuously verified, stopping the attack.

How to Implement Segmentation and Zero Trust Together

🔒 Step 1: Map Your Network

Identify all connected IIoT devices, controllers, and access points

Determine which systems actually need to communicate

🔒 Step 2: Segment the Network

Use VLANs, firewalls, and IDMZs to create strong boundaries

Implement micro-segmentation to limit device-to-device access

🔒 Step 3: Apply Zero Trust Policies

Require strict authentication for every connection

Continuously monitor and validate all access requests

🔒 Step 4: Monitor and Adapt

Use intrusion detection systems (IDS) to watch for suspicious activity

Continuously update security rules based on new threats

Final Thoughts: No More Open Kitchens, No More Flat Networks

The old "trust but verify" approach is dead. Attackers don't knock on the front door anymore—they sneak in through an unlocked window, disguise themselves as staff, and go straight for the valuables.

A strong segmentation strategy and a Zero Trust model are the best ways to stop them. It's time to lock down our IIoT environments like a high-security vault—because if attackers can't move freely, they can't take down an entire factory. 🚀

3.3 Identifying and Securing Exposed IIoT Devices with Network Scanning

Finding Your IIoT Devices Before Hackers Do

Imagine you just moved into a new house. You lock the front door, set up a security system, and feel pretty good about things—until your neighbor casually mentions that your basement window is wide open and your garage door doesn't even have a lock. Now you're picturing burglars walking right in and helping themselves to your snacks and TV.

That's exactly what happens with IIoT devices when companies don't know what's exposed. You can't secure what you don't know exists—and trust me, in most industrial networks, there are plenty of forgotten devices, unpatched controllers, and open ports just waiting for an attacker to find.

The bad guys are already looking—using tools like Shodan and Censys to scan for exposed industrial systems. If you're not scanning your own network first, you're basically playing a high-stakes game of hide and seek... but the hackers aren't the ones hiding.

How IIoT Devices Get Exposed Without You Knowing

Industrial networks weren't designed for always-on connectivity like today's IT environments. But as factories, power plants, and logistics hubs rush to integrate IIoT, more devices are getting connected—and in many cases, they're connected badly.

Here's how IIoT devices end up exposed:

Misconfigured Firewalls – Someone accidentally leaves a port open to the internet, making your SCADA system as accessible as a public Wi-Fi network.

Default Credentials – IIoT vendors love to ship devices with default usernames and passwords like "admin/admin" (which hackers know by heart).

Shadow IT – An engineer installs a wireless gateway for remote monitoring without telling security. Surprise! Now attackers have a backdoor.

Aging Legacy Systems – Many ICS and SCADA devices weren't built for security but are still running in critical environments.

Third-Party Integrations – A supplier's remote access system gets compromised, and suddenly, your industrial robots are under new management.

Real-World Example:

In 2021, a water treatment plant in Florida was hacked remotely because an old TeamViewer account was still active. The attackers tried to increase the lye levels in the water—a serious public safety risk. The breach was only caught by an observant employee. A simple network scan would have detected the open connection before an attacker did.

Step 1: Identify All Connected IIoT Devices (Before Someone Else Does)

The first step in securing IIoT devices is knowing what's actually on your network. If you think your environment is fully mapped out, think again—in my 20 years of cybersecurity, I've never seen a company that actually had 100% visibility.

🔍 How to Scan for IIoT Devices

✅ Passive Network Scanning (Safe but Limited)

Uses traffic monitoring to detect connected devices without disrupting operations

Good for sensitive environments where uptime is critical

Tools: Nozomi Networks, Claroty, Dragos

✅ Active Network Scanning (More Aggressive but Detailed)

Sends probes to identify devices, open ports, and vulnerabilities

Can cause instability in fragile ICS/SCADA systems (test carefully!)

Tools: Nmap, ZMap, Tenable Nessus

✅ OSINT Recon (What Hackers See)

Shodan, Censys, and ZoomEye scan the internet for exposed IIoT devices

Run your own searches before attackers do to see what's publicly visible

Example Shodan query:

title:"SCADA" country:"US"

📹 Pro Tip: Set up alerts in Shodan or Censys for your organization's IP addresses. If something suddenly appears exposed on the internet, you'll know before it's too late.

Step 2: Lock Down and Secure Exposed Devices

Once you've identified what's out there, it's time to fix the mess.

🔒 Securing IIoT Devices from Hackers

✅ Close Unnecessary Open Ports

If an IIoT device doesn't need internet access, block it!

Common risky ports:

502 (Modbus)

47808 (BACnet)

1911 (Tridium Niagara)

44818 (EtherNet/IP)

✅ Change Default Credentials (Seriously, Just Do It)

Check if any devices still use default usernames and passwords

If the manufacturer doesn't allow password changes, consider replacing the device

✅ Use Network Segmentation (No More Flat Networks!)

Place IIoT devices in isolated VLANs

Separate IT and OT environments with a firewall or an industrial DMZ

✅ Enable Logging and Monitor Activity

Set up SIEM (Security Information & Event Management) alerts for suspicious access

If an IIoT device suddenly starts talking to an unknown IP in Russia, investigate!

🔍 Real-World Example:

An energy company found that over 1,000 of its industrial sensors were exposed with open ports. Worse, they were using default passwords that had been leaked online. After locking down access and forcing password changes, they avoided what could have been a catastrophic cyber attack.

Step 3: Automate Network Scanning and Continuous Monitoring

Finding and fixing vulnerabilities once isn't enough—you need ongoing visibility.

☐ Essential Tools for Continuous Monitoring

Security Onion – Open-source threat detection for IIoT networks

Snort or Suricata – Intrusion detection systems (IDS) to detect attacks in real time

CyberX – Specializes in ICS/SCADA monitoring

☐ Set up automated scans to check for new vulnerabilities weekly or monthly. If a new IIoT device appears on the network unexpectedly, find out why—fast.

Final Thoughts: If You're Not Scanning, You're Already Compromised

IIoT security isn't about guessing—it's about knowing. You can't protect what you haven't identified, and if you're not regularly scanning your network, attackers are doing it for you.

The Playbook for Securing IIoT Devices:

✅ Find every connected device—don't assume, scan!

✅ Check for exposed ports, weak passwords, and outdated firmware

✅ Segment IIoT networks and restrict unnecessary access

✅ Monitor in real-time and set alerts for suspicious activity

At the end of the day, securing IIoT isn't about making things impossible for hackers—it's about making their job so frustrating they give up and move on. So start scanning, start securing, and stop giving cybercriminals free access to your network. 🚀

3.4 Detecting and Preventing MITM and Packet Injection Attacks

Man-in-the-Middle Attacks: When Hackers Eavesdrop on Your Industrial Secrets

Picture this: You're sitting at your favorite coffee shop, casually using public Wi-Fi to check your emails. Little do you know, a hacker sitting three tables away is intercepting your traffic, reading your emails, and maybe even injecting fake messages into your inbox. Now, imagine that instead of your inbox, it's a SCADA system controlling a power grid.

Welcome to the world of Man-in-the-Middle (MITM) and Packet Injection attacks—where attackers secretly position themselves between two devices to eavesdrop, manipulate, or completely hijack communications. In the industrial world, where IIoT, SCADA, and PLCs rely on unsecured legacy protocols, MITM attacks are frighteningly easy to pull off. And if you're not watching for them, you may never know they're happening.

How MITM and Packet Injection Attacks Work in IIoT

Unlike IT environments where TLS encryption and secure authentication are common, OT networks are a different beast. Many IIoT systems use protocols like Modbus, DNP3, and PROFINET, which were designed in the pre-cybersecurity era, meaning they trust everything. That's bad news if an attacker gets in.

Common MITM Attack Techniques in IIoT

● ARP Spoofing (The Classic MITM Trick)

Attackers trick devices on the network into thinking their machine is the trusted gateway, intercepting and modifying traffic in real time.

🏛 **Real-World Example**: A researcher demonstrated an ARP spoofing attack on a smart factory, allowing them to manipulate sensor data. The factory's automated systems reacted to false readings, causing production line slowdowns and errors—all because an attacker was silently altering traffic.

● Rogue Access Points (Fake Wi-Fi Networks)

An attacker sets up a malicious Wi-Fi access point with a name similar to a trusted network. Employees or engineers unknowingly connect, and boom—all their traffic is now passing through the hacker's laptop.

🔊 **Danger Zone:** Many modern factories use wireless sensors and mobile HMIs—which means if attackers control the Wi-Fi, they control the industrial network.

● **Packet Injection (Tampering with Industrial Data)**

Instead of just eavesdropping, hackers take it a step further by modifying or injecting malicious commands into the communication stream.

🔊 **Terrifying Example**: In 2010, Stuxnet became famous for modifying SCADA commands. The malware intercepted legitimate instructions to centrifuges at an Iranian nuclear facility, replacing them with commands that sped up and slowed down the equipment until it self-destructed. This is the ultimate nightmare scenario for any industrial facility.

Detecting MITM and Packet Injection in IIoT Networks

So, how do you know if someone's lurking in the middle of your network, manipulating your traffic? Here's how to spot an attack before it causes real damage.

🔍 **Signs You Might Be Under a MITM Attack**

✓ **Unexpected Network Latency** – If data that normally travels at milliseconds suddenly takes much longer, someone could be intercepting and relaying it.
✓ **Duplicate MAC Addresses on the Network** – ARP spoofing often creates conflicting MAC addresses (your network scanner should alert you).
✓ **Devices Connecting to Unexpected Wi-Fi Networks** – Watch for rogue access points that look similar to your factory's actual network.
✓ **Mismatched Data in Logs** – If SCADA logs show a machine running at 50% capacity, but sensors say it's at 100%, data may be manipulated in transit.

☐ **Tools for MITM Attack Detection**

Wireshark – Analyze packet traffic and detect anomalies in industrial protocols.

ARPwatch – Monitors ARP traffic and alerts when a potential spoofing attack occurs.

Snort or Suricata – Detects MITM and packet injection attempts in real-time.

Zigbee Sniffers – Useful for detecting MITM attacks in wireless IIoT networks.

⚙ **Pro Tip**: Use network baselining—record normal traffic behavior so you can immediately spot anything suspicious. If an HMI usually communicates with a PLC every 10 seconds, and suddenly it's every second, something's wrong.

Preventing MITM and Packet Injection Attacks

Now that we know the dangers, let's talk defense.

🔒 **Step 1: Enforce Strong Network Segmentation**

Keep IT and OT networks separate—a hacker shouldn't be able to pivot from your office Wi-Fi into your SCADA system.

Use VLANs to isolate critical IIoT devices.

🔒 **Step 2: Implement Strong Authentication & Encryption**

Many industrial protocols don't have built-in security—but you can still wrap them in VPNs, IPSec, or TLS tunnels.

Enable Mutual Authentication – This ensures that only trusted devices can communicate with each other.

⚙ **Reality Check**: Many IIoT devices don't support encryption by default—which is why attackers love them. If your vendor doesn't offer encryption, pressure them to update their firmware or switch vendors.

🔒 **Step 3: Use ARP Spoofing Protection**

Enable Dynamic ARP Inspection (DAI) on network switches—this blocks malicious ARP spoofing attacks.

Monitor ARP tables for unexpected changes.

🔒 **Step 4: Deploy Industrial Firewalls with Deep Packet Inspection (DPI)**

Standard firewalls aren't enough—you need DPI firewalls that understand Modbus, DNP3, and OPC-UA to block malicious injections.

🔒 Step 5: Physically Secure Wireless Networks

If you use Wi-Fi or LPWAN (LoRa, Zigbee, etc.), make sure rogue devices can't easily connect.

Change default SSIDs and disable weak encryption (WEP, WPA1—just no).

Use MAC address whitelisting for trusted industrial devices.

Final Thoughts: MITM Attacks Are Silent Killers—Stay Ahead of Them

Hackers love MITM and packet injection attacks because they don't need to break into your network—they just manipulate what's already there. And in industrial environments where legacy protocols trust everything, MITM is one of the easiest and most devastating attacks.

💡 Key Takeaways:

✓ If your IIoT network isn't encrypted, assume it's already compromised.

✓ Monitor for ARP spoofing, rogue Wi-Fi access points, and unusual traffic patterns.

✓ Use industrial-grade firewalls with DPI to block packet injection attempts.

✓ Never trust default settings—harden your IIoT infrastructure before attackers do.

At the end of the day, MITM attacks are like having an invisible spy in your factory—but with the right detection and prevention strategies, you can make sure that spy gets caught before they cause real damage. 🚀

3.5 Best Practices for Securing ICS and OT Networks

Welcome to the Cyber Wild West of OT Networks

If IT networks are like a modern-day fortified castle, then OT networks are like a Wild West town where everyone leaves their doors unlocked and hopes for the best. The reason? Legacy systems, weak security, and a 'safety first, security later' mindset.

I once asked an old-school plant engineer why their SCADA system was still running Windows XP, and they replied, "Because it still works!" Yeah... but so does my grandma's 20-year-old microwave, and I still wouldn't trust it to heat my dinner without setting the house on fire. Just because something works doesn't mean it's secure.

And that, my friend, is the challenge with securing Industrial Control Systems (ICS) and Operational Technology (OT) networks. It's not just about patching systems—it's about changing the entire approach to security while keeping industrial operations running smoothly.

Understanding the Unique Challenges of ICS and OT Security

Before we jump into best practices, let's acknowledge the elephant in the room—securing OT isn't like securing IT. If you try to apply traditional IT security rules to an OT environment without considering operational impacts, you're going to break things fast.

Key Differences Between IT and OT Security

Factor	IT Security	OT Security
Primary Focus	Data protection (Confidentiality)	System uptime & reliability (Availability)
Patch Management	Regular updates & patches	Often delayed or **not possible** due to operational risks
Security Tools	Firewalls, antivirus, IDS/IPS	Industrial firewalls, **deep packet inspection**, and anomaly detection
Downtime Acceptability	Some downtime is manageable	**Even seconds of downtime can cost millions**
Device Lifespan	3-5 years	**20+ years (hello, Windows XP)**

These differences mean that blindly applying IT security practices to ICS systems can cause more harm than good. Instead, we need OT-specific security strategies.

Best Practices for Securing ICS and OT Networks

1⃞ Network Segmentation: Keep IT and OT Separate

One of the biggest mistakes industrial organizations make? Blending IT and OT networks like a bad cocktail. When OT devices connect directly to the internet or corporate IT networks, you invite hackers to the party.

How to Segment Your OT Network Properly

✅ **Air-Gap Critical Systems** – If it doesn't need external connectivity, keep it isolated.

✅ **Use the Purdue Model** – This security framework divides ICS/OT networks into layers (Enterprise, DMZ, Operations, Control, Field).

✅ **Firewall Everything** – Strictly control traffic between IT and OT using industrial-grade firewalls with deep packet inspection (DPI) for Modbus, DNP3, and OPC-UA traffic.

✅ **Implement DMZs** – Don't let IT users directly access OT systems. Use a secure proxy or jump host.

📹 Real-World Horror Story:

A major oil refinery was hit by ransomware when an employee's infected laptop from IT was plugged into the OT network for maintenance. The result? Production shut down for 48 hours, costing millions.

2⃞ Enforce Strong Access Controls (No More Shared Passwords!)

OT networks are notorious for weak authentication. Hardcoded credentials? Default passwords? Shared logins? Yep, all common. And hackers love it.

How to Lock Down Access Properly

✅ **Use Multi-Factor Authentication (MFA)** – If it's connected to the internet, MFA should be mandatory.

✅ **Eliminate Default Credentials** – Change every default username and password.

✅ **Implement Role-Based Access Control (RBAC)** – Operators, engineers, and admins should only have access to what they need.

✅ **Monitor and Audit Logins** – If a maintenance account logs in at 3 AM from a foreign IP, you have a problem.

Fun Fact: In a 2021 security audit, researchers found over 56,000 ICS/OT devices exposed online using default passwords.

3 Secure Remote Access (Because Hackers Love RDP)

Since the pandemic, remote access to OT networks has skyrocketed—but most companies set it up without security in mind. Attackers know this, and they're brute-forcing RDP, VPNs, and exposed VNC servers like there's no tomorrow.

How to Secure Remote Access

✅ **Use VPNs with Strong Authentication** – No plain old RDP or VNC exposed to the internet.
✅ **Require Jump Hosts** – Engineers and vendors should connect through a controlled jump server, not directly to ICS devices.
✅ **Enable Session Recording** – Keep logs of all remote access sessions to detect any suspicious behavior.
✅ **Whitelist IPs for Remote Access** – If someone tries to log in from a random country, block them.

Scary Reality Check:

Hackers gained access to a water treatment plant in Florida by remotely logging into an exposed system with a weak password. They tried to poison the water supply by increasing lye levels. Luckily, a vigilant operator caught the change in time.

4 Monitor and Detect Anomalies (Because OT Attacks Are Sneaky)

If you can't see what's happening on your OT network, how will you detect an attack? Traditional IT security solutions don't work well in OT, so you need industrial-focused monitoring.

How to Monitor OT Networks for Threats

✅ **Deploy Industrial IDS/IPS Solutions** – Use tools like Nozomi Networks, Dragos, or Claroty to detect ICS-specific threats.
✅ **Set Up Behavioral Anomaly Detection** – If a PLC suddenly starts sending data to an unknown IP, something's wrong.

✓ **Implement Logging and SIEM Integration** – OT logs should be fed into a security operations center (SOC) for real-time monitoring.

📖 **Example**: A security team detected a new, unauthorized PLC on their network. Turns out, an attacker had installed a rogue device to intercept SCADA traffic.

5️⃣ Patch and Harden Everything (Even if You Can't Patch)

OT systems are infamous for never being updated—because taking them offline for patching could disrupt production. But you can't ignore vulnerabilities forever.

How to Secure OT Systems Without Breaking Operations

✓ **Use Virtual Patching** – If you can't patch, use network-based intrusion prevention (IPS) to block known exploits.
✓ **Lock Down Unused Services** – If a device doesn't need a service (like SMB or Telnet), disable it.
✓ **Whitelist Applications** – Prevent unauthorized software from running on industrial PCs and HMIs.

📷 **Nightmare Scenario:**

WannaCry ransomware spread like wildfire through unpatched Windows machines, shutting down automotive plants, hospitals, and industrial systems worldwide.

Final Thoughts: Securing OT is a Marathon, Not a Sprint

OT security isn't about locking everything down overnight—it's about taking continuous steps to reduce risk without disrupting operations. Every firewall rule, access control update, and patch you apply makes attackers' jobs harder.

💡 **Key Takeaways:**

✓ **Keep IT and OT separate**—no more flat networks!
✓ **Secure remote access**—VPNs, MFA, and jump hosts only!
✓ **Monitor everything**—because attacks aren't always obvious!
✓ **Harden systems**—because attackers love unpatched devices!

Bottom line? If you don't secure your ICS and OT networks now, attackers will do it for you—but not in the way you'd like. 😺

Chapter 4: Reconnaissance and Attack Surface Mapping

Ever wonder how hackers find vulnerable IIoT devices before launching an attack? Spoiler alert: It's easier than you think. With tools like Shodan and Censys, attackers can scan the internet for exposed SCADA systems from the comfort of their couch. The worst part? Many organizations don't even realize their industrial devices are publicly accessible until it's too late. If your IIoT infrastructure is out in the open, you might as well put up a neon sign that says: "Hack Me!"

This chapter explores the reconnaissance phase of industrial hacking, focusing on how attackers map out vulnerabilities in IIoT environments. We'll examine passive and active reconnaissance techniques, fingerprinting SCADA components, and the role of OSINT (Open-Source Intelligence) in industrial cyber threats. Finally, we'll discuss hardening strategies to prevent unauthorized discovery and reconnaissance of IIoT systems.

4.1 Identifying Exposed Industrial IoT Devices via OSINT (Shodan, Censys)

Welcome to the World of OSINT: Where Hackers Don't Need to Hack

If breaking into a system was like breaking into a house, then Open Source Intelligence (OSINT) is like finding the homeowner's spare key under the doormat. And trust me, industrial networks have a lot of doormats.

Hackers don't always need zero-day exploits or nation-state budgets to compromise an Industrial IoT (IIoT) system. Sometimes, they just Google it. Well, not literally Google— but they do use specialized search engines like Shodan and Censys, which map out and index internet-exposed devices.

I once showed a factory owner that his SCADA system was publicly exposed on Shodan. His reaction? "Wait, what's a Shodan?" □ That's when I knew we had a serious problem.

So, let's dive in and see how attackers find your exposed IIoT devices before you do— and more importantly, how to stop them.

What is OSINT, and Why Should You Care?

OSINT 101: Spying Without Breaking the Law

Open Source Intelligence (OSINT) is the practice of gathering information from publicly available sources. This includes:

✅ Search engines (Google, Bing, DuckDuckGo)

✅ IoT search engines (Shodan, Censys, ZoomEye)

✅ Public forums and GitHub repositories

✅ Social media and job postings (Yes, LinkedIn job descriptions can reveal industrial tech stacks!)

✅ Leaked credentials on the dark web

Why Industrial IoT Devices are OSINT Goldmines

Industrial devices weren't designed for internet exposure. Most ICS/SCADA systems, smart factory controllers, and remote access gateways were built with functionality first, security second (or never). That means:

✗ Weak authentication (default passwords, no MFA)

✗ Unpatched vulnerabilities in legacy systems

✗ Direct exposure to the internet without firewalls

✗ Protocols that were never meant to be secure (Modbus, DNP3, MQTT, OPC-UA, etc.)

A single search on Shodan or Censys can reveal thousands of vulnerable IIoT devices just waiting for someone to poke at them.

Shodan and Censys: The Search Engines of the Dark Side

🔍 Shodan: The "Google" of the Internet of Things

Shodan is a search engine that scans and indexes internet-connected devices, including:

✓☐ SCADA systems (Wonderware, Siemens, Rockwell Automation)
✓☐ Industrial control devices (PLCs, HMIs, RTUs)

✓☐ Security cameras, routers, smart sensors

✓☐ Power grids, water treatment plants, and factories (Yes, it's terrifying.)

Example: Searching for Exposed ICS Devices on Shodan

Try searching:

SCADA country:US

or

port:502 modbus

This will show all publicly accessible SCADA systems and Modbus devices in the U.S. Scary, right? ☹

Other Shodan Filters for IIoT & ICS:

port:44818 (Rockwell Automation Ethernet/IP devices)

port:102 (Siemens S7 PLCs)

port:1911 (Tridium Niagara Framework)

port:2404 (IEC 60870-5-104 power grid control systems)

product:"MQTT" (Finds exposed MQTT brokers)

📷 Real-World Horror Story:

A security researcher once found a water treatment plant's SCADA system fully accessible on Shodan—with no password protection. An attacker could have manipulated chemical levels in drinking water. Let that sink in. ☐

☐☐ Censys: The Deep-Diving Alternative to Shodan

Censys is similar to Shodan but focuses on richer metadata about exposed devices. It scans the internet and provides detailed reports on:

✓☐ TLS certificates (useful for fingerprinting industrial web interfaces)

✓☐ IoT firmware versions (which may have known vulnerabilities)
✓☐ Network services running on IIoT devices

Example: Finding Exposed ICS Devices on Censys

Try searching:

services.service_name: "Modbus"

or

80.http.get.title: "SCADA"

This will reveal public-facing industrial systems with web interfaces—many of which still use default credentials.

🔍 Real-World Example:

A Censys search once uncovered an entire smart factory's control panel accessible online, including temperature, production speed, and emergency shutdown controls. Just one exposed login page away from disaster.

How to Identify & Secure Your Own Exposed IIoT Devices

1☐ Check Your Own Industrial Devices on Shodan & Censys

☐ **Before an attacker finds them, YOU should.**

Go to Shodan.io and search for your:

Company name

Factory's IP range

Specific ICS vendors you use (e.g., Siemens, Rockwell, Schneider)

Use Censys.io to find TLS certificates linked to your industrial systems.

Scan for exposed industrial protocols (Modbus, DNP3, MQTT, etc.).

2️⃣ Lock Down Remote Access Immediately

✅ Use VPNs with MFA instead of exposing industrial systems.

✅ Disable remote access if it's not absolutely necessary.

✅ Use firewall rules to restrict access to trusted IPs only.

3️⃣ Change Default Credentials & Use Strong Authentication

🔓 Hardcoded and default passwords are an open invitation to attackers.

✅ Change every factory-default password immediately.

✅ Implement Multi-Factor Authentication (MFA) for remote access.

4️⃣ Hide IIoT Devices from Public Scanning

✅ Disable unnecessary ports and services.

✅ Use industrial firewalls to filter traffic.

✅ Deploy honeypots (fake decoy devices) to detect unauthorized scanning.

Final Thoughts: The Best Defense is Knowing You're Exposed

If your IIoT and industrial systems are online, someone is looking at them—and they may not have good intentions. OSINT tools like Shodan and Censys make it easier than ever for attackers to find vulnerable IIoT devices.

💡 Key Takeaways:

✓ Hackers don't need advanced exploits—they just search for exposed devices.
✓ Shodan and Censys are powerful tools for both attackers and defenders.
✓ Check YOUR company's industrial exposure before someone else does.
✓ Secure remote access, enforce strong passwords, and block unnecessary ports.

Bottom line? If your IIoT system is online, you better be 100% sure it's locked down. Because if it's not… Shodan will tell the world. 🌍

4.2 Passive and Active Recon Techniques for Smart Factories

Spying on Smart Factories: The Art of Reconnaissance

Before an attacker (or a security professional like us) breaks into an industrial network, they first need to know what they're dealing with. And that's where reconnaissance comes into play.

Think of it like scouting a bank before a heist—except instead of looking for security cameras and guard shifts, we're mapping out exposed IP addresses, unpatched SCADA systems, and forgotten factory floor devices.

Smart factories are loaded with sensors, IoT devices, industrial control systems (ICS), and wireless networks. The problem? Most of them were built with little to no cybersecurity in mind. That's why both ethical hackers and cybercriminals use passive and active recon techniques to uncover weaknesses.

In this section, we'll dive into how attackers gather intelligence on smart factories—and how you can detect and stop them before they strike.

Passive vs. Active Recon: What's the Difference?

Reconnaissance techniques fall into two main categories:

Recon Type	What It Means	Risk of Detection
Passive Recon	Gathering data without directly interacting with the target	Low (stealthy)
Active Recon	Probing and scanning the target network directly	High (easier to detect)

A good attacker always starts with passive recon—why ring the alarm before you even step inside the building?

Passive Recon: Watching Without Touching

Passive reconnaissance is all about collecting information without touching the target system directly. This means using public sources, search engines, leaked credentials, and metadata to build a full picture of the factory's attack surface.

1⃞ Open Source Intelligence (OSINT) Gathering

OSINT is the hacker's best friend. With just a few searches, you can find industrial devices, employee credentials, and even network configurations—all publicly available!

Shodan, Censys, ZoomEye → Find exposed ICS/SCADA devices

Google Dorking → Search for leaked credentials, PDFs, and configuration files

GitHub & Pastebin → Look for exposed passwords or API keys

Social Media & LinkedIn → Identify employees, technologies used, and key targets

💡 **Example**: Searching for "SCADA login" filetype:pdf on Google might reveal a factory's user manual, complete with default passwords.

2⃞ DNS, WHOIS, and IP Intelligence

Even if a factory doesn't publicly list its internal network, there are ways to find its internet-facing assets:

WHOIS Lookup → Reveals the factory's registered domains & IP ranges

DNS Reconnaissance → Identifies subdomains & hidden systems

Reverse IP Lookups → Maps multiple factory assets hosted on the same IP

💡 **Example**: A misconfigured subdomain like vpn.factoryname.com might expose an unsecured remote access portal. Oops.

3⃞ Metadata Analysis (Leaked Clues in Files!)

A single PDF, Word document, or image uploaded by a company could expose internal IP addresses, usernames, or software versions.

FOCA & ExifTool → Extract metadata from documents & images

Check document authors → Sometimes, employees use their work usernames in file metadata (which gives us valid usernames for brute-force attacks).

💡 **Example**: An attacker finds an internal PLC configuration file uploaded by an employee—complete with IP addresses of all factory floor devices. Game over.

Active Recon: Poking the Factory to See What Breaks

Once an attacker has a list of potential targets, they move to active reconnaissance—which means interacting with the network directly to map out vulnerabilities.

This is riskier, but it provides real-time, accurate data on what systems are running.

1️⃣ Network Scanning: The Hacker's X-Ray Vision

Active scanning tools send packets to the target network to identify live devices, open ports, and running services.

Nmap → The ultimate network scanning tool

Masscan → Super-fast port scanning

Zmap → Internet-wide scanning for specific services (like MQTT or Modbus)

💡 **Example**: Running Nmap -p 502 -sV factory-ip might reveal an unprotected Modbus device, giving direct control over industrial machinery. Yikes.

2️⃣ ICS & SCADA Protocol Fingerprinting

Smart factories run on specialized industrial protocols that weren't designed for security. Attackers can fingerprint these protocols to identify specific devices.

Modbus, DNP3, IEC 61850, OPC-UA → Common SCADA/ICS protocols

PLCScan, ModScan, pymodbus → Tools to enumerate industrial devices

Wireshark & tshark → Capture live industrial network traffic

💡 **Example**: A hacker sends a simple Modbus request to an exposed PLC. If it responds? They now know it's a live, vulnerable device.

3️⃣ Sniffing & MITM Attacks

If an attacker gains network access, they can intercept & manipulate industrial traffic.

Wireshark → Capture & analyze SCADA network traffic

Ettercap & Bettercap → Perform Man-in-the-Middle (MITM) attacks

ModbusProxy & MBLogic → Tamper with real-time Modbus traffic

💡 **Example**: An attacker uses MITM on an OPC-UA connection to modify sensor readings in real-time, fooling factory operators into making bad decisions.

Defending Against Recon: How to Hide Your Smart Factory

Now that we know how attackers gather intelligence, how do we stop them?

✅ **Monitor OSINT leaks** → Regularly check Shodan, Censys, and Google Dorks for exposed assets

✅ **Harden remote access** → Close unused ports, enforce MFA, and use VPNs instead of public logins

✅ **Implement network segmentation** → Separate IT and OT networks

✅ **Use deception techniques** → Deploy honeypots to catch recon attempts

✅ **Monitor network traffic** → Use intrusion detection systems (IDS) to flag abnormal scans

Final Thoughts: If You Can See It, Hackers Can Too

Reconnaissance is the first step in every cyber attack. Whether it's OSINT digging through leaked PDFs or active scanning for open ports, attackers will always find the easiest way in.

💡 **Key Takeaways:**

✓□ Passive recon is stealthy (OSINT, Shodan, metadata analysis)
✓□ Active recon is riskier but more detailed (port scanning, MITM, SCADA fingerprinting)
✓□ If you don't know your own attack surface, attackers will find it first

So, before the bad guys scan your smart factory, make sure you do it first—and lock it down. Because nothing ruins an attacker's day like finding nothing to exploit. ☺

4.3 Fingerprinting ICS and SCADA Components for Vulnerability Assessment

Identifying Industrial Devices: Like Picking Locks, but Ethical

Imagine a burglar casing a neighborhood. They don't just smash the first window they see—they check for unlocked doors, weak locks, and security cameras before making a move. Well, cyber attackers do the same thing when they target Industrial Control Systems (ICS) and SCADA networks.

This is called fingerprinting, and in the industrial world, it's shockingly easy to do. Why? Because many ICS/SCADA components scream their identity to the world like an overeager intern handing out business cards.

Hackers (and security professionals like us) love fingerprinting because it helps us:

🔍 Identify specific industrial devices (PLCs, RTUs, HMIs)

🔍 Find out firmware and software versions (so we know which exploits to use)

🔍 Map out the network structure (so we know where the juicy targets are)

In this chapter, we'll explore how attackers fingerprint ICS and SCADA systems, what tools they use, and—most importantly—how to stop them before they exploit the vulnerabilities they find.

Why Fingerprinting is a Big Deal in Industrial Networks

Unlike IT networks, where fingerprinting might just expose an email server or a web application, ICS fingerprinting can reveal life-or-death control systems that regulate power grids, water treatment plants, and factory automation.

Example:

A hacker fingerprints a Siemens S7-1200 PLC running an outdated firmware version.

They look up known vulnerabilities and find an exploit that allows remote command execution.

Congratulations, they now have full control over industrial machinery. 🎉 (Bad news for the factory, though.)

Passive Fingerprinting: When the Target Gives Up Info Without a Fight

Passive fingerprinting is non-intrusive—attackers just listen and observe, rather than actively probing the system.

1️ OSINT and Search Engine Hunting

Attackers don't even need to touch the target network to gather valuable information. A few searches can expose publicly accessible ICS devices:

🔍 **Shodan & Censys** → Find internet-exposed SCADA systems

🔍 **Google Dorking** → Search for ICS manuals, default passwords, and network configurations

🔍 **GitHub & Pastebin** → Find leaked credentials or industrial software

💡 **Example**: Searching "PLC password site:pastebin.com" might reveal a careless employee's hardcoded credentials for a factory's control system. Oops.

2️⃣ Network Traffic Analysis

Many ICS/SCADA devices leak information in network traffic—sometimes even in plaintext. Attackers use:

Wireshark & Tshark → To capture industrial protocol traffic

NetFlow & Zeek → To analyze network behavior & identify ICS devices

💡 **Example**: A hacker monitoring network traffic sees Modbus TCP requests coming from a specific IP. They now know:

✓ The factory uses Modbus for control

✓ The IP address belongs to a PLC or RTU

✓ The system might not have authentication (since Modbus has none by default)

This means an attacker is already halfway to full control. Yikes.

Active Fingerprinting: When Attackers Poke the System to See What Moves

Once an attacker has passively mapped out potential targets, they move to active fingerprinting—which involves sending requests and analyzing responses.

This is louder and riskier (admins might detect the activity), but it provides direct confirmation of vulnerable devices.

1️⃣ Port Scanning for ICS Services

The first step is scanning for common ICS/SCADA ports:

Protocol	Port	Used For
Modbus	502	PLC Communication
DNP3	20000	Electric Grid Control
OPC-UA	4840	Industrial Data Exchange
BACnet	47808	Building Automation
PROFINET	34962	Factory Automation

Attackers use tools like:

Nmap → To scan for ICS devices

Masscan → To quickly scan thousands of devices at once

💡 **Example**: Running nmap -p 502 --script modbus-discover target-ip might reveal a Modbus PLC that allows unrestricted access. Game over.

2️ Banner Grabbing: Devices That Introduce Themselves

Some ICS devices announce their model, firmware, and software versions in their responses. Attackers use:

Netcat & Telnet → To connect directly to industrial devices

Nmap Scripting Engine (NSE) → To grab ICS service banners

Metasploit Auxiliary Modules → To fingerprint SCADA systems

💡 **Example: A hacker runs:**

nc target-ip 502

The Modbus PLC responds with its firmware version. If it's outdated, the attacker knows which exploit to use. Oops.

3⃞ Protocol-Specific Probing

Some tools are built specifically for fingerprinting industrial protocols:

ModScan & pymodbus → Identify Modbus PLCs

PLCScan → Find programmable logic controllers (PLCs)

PROFINET Scanner → Discover factory automation devices

S7comm Scanner → Fingerprint Siemens PLCs

💡 **Example**: Using pymodbus to send a test Modbus request, a hacker confirms the PLC exists and accepts remote commands. Uh-oh.

Defending Against ICS & SCADA Fingerprinting

If attackers can fingerprint your ICS network, they can hack it. Here's how to stop them in their tracks:

✅ **Hide ICS systems from the internet** → Close unnecessary ports, use firewalls, and disable direct external access

✅ **Use Network Segmentation** → Separate IT and OT networks with strict access controls

✅ **Deploy Intrusion Detection Systems (IDS)** → Use Zeek, Suricata, or Snort to detect ICS scanning attempts

✅ **Encrypt Industrial Protocols** → Where possible, implement TLS for OPC-UA & VPNs for remote access

☑ **Regularly Update Firmware** → Patch known vulnerabilities before attackers exploit them

☑ **Use Deception & Honeypots** → Deploy fake ICS systems to trick and track attackers

Final Thoughts: If It Talks, It Can Be Fingerprinted

Fingerprinting is the first step in hacking an industrial system. Attackers use passive and active techniques to identify vulnerable PLCs, RTUs, and SCADA components—and if you're not monitoring, you'll never even know they were there.

💡 **Key Takeaways:**

✓☐ Passive recon is stealthy (Shodan, network monitoring, metadata leaks)
✓☐ Active recon is riskier but reveals more info (port scans, banner grabbing, ICS probes)
✓☐ If attackers can fingerprint your ICS network, they can exploit it

So, scan your own systems before the bad guys do. Because nothing ruins a hacker's day more than finding out you're already one step ahead. ☺

4.4 Side-Channel Attacks and Physical Recon on Industrial Devices

The Sneaky Art of Stealing Secrets Without Hacking

Ever tried to guess someone's ATM PIN by watching their fingers move? Or figured out someone's password just by listening to their keyboard clicks? Congratulations! You've dabbled in side-channel attacks—where hackers don't break into a system directly but instead observe, measure, and infer information from unintended leaks.

Now, apply that to Industrial IoT (IIoT) and SCADA systems, and things get real messy. Hackers don't always need a fancy zero-day exploit to take over a power plant. Sometimes, all it takes is a cheap oscilloscope, a power meter, or even a smartphone microphone to extract data from an industrial device without ever touching its code.

And then there's physical recon, where attackers literally walk into a factory, take notes, snap pictures, and identify weak points—like a bad guy in a heist movie scouting a bank vault. Spoiler alert: Many industrial sites make this shockingly easy by leaving devices exposed, using weak locks, and never questioning a dude in a reflective vest.

Welcome to the world of side-channel attacks and physical reconnaissance—where hackers don't hack… they just watch, listen, and steal data in plain sight.

Side-Channel Attacks: Hacking Without Breaking In

Unlike traditional cyberattacks, side-channel attacks (SCAs) don't exploit software vulnerabilities. Instead, they rely on physical and electrical signals that devices give off during operation. These leaks—like power fluctuations, electromagnetic emissions, and even sound—can reveal sensitive data about what the device is doing.

1⃞ Power Analysis Attacks: Watching the Energy Flow

Industrial devices, like PLCs and embedded controllers, consume different amounts of power depending on the operations they perform. Hackers can measure these fluctuations to extract cryptographic keys or infer process data.

🔍 Types of Power Analysis Attacks:

Simple Power Analysis (SPA): A hacker measures power usage while a device encrypts data and identifies patterns.

Differential Power Analysis (DPA): By collecting and comparing thousands of power traces, attackers can extract encryption keys.

💡 Example:

An attacker places a small power meter on a factory's control panel and logs voltage fluctuations over time. Using statistical analysis, they recover the AES encryption key used to secure communications between the PLC and SCADA system. Boom. Factory compromised.

2⃞ Electromagnetic (EM) Emanations: When Devices Talk Through the Air

Did you know that every electronic device emits electromagnetic waves? Hackers do. And they can use special antennas and software-defined radios (SDRs) to pick up these emissions and reconstruct what's happening inside an ICS device.

🔍 Tools of the Trade:

HackRF One & RTL-SDR: Low-cost SDRs for sniffing EM signals.

TEMPEST attacks: Military-grade spying technique that reconstructs screen displays from leaked EM radiation.

Faraday cages: The best defense (but also super expensive).

💡 Example:

A hacker in a nearby van uses an SDR to capture EM signals from a SCADA workstation. By analyzing the emissions, they recover keystrokes and passwords typed by the operator—without ever touching the network. That's some James Bond-level hacking right there.

3️⃣ Acoustic Cryptanalysis: Listening to Data Leaks

Yes, hackers can literally listen to your devices to steal secrets. Many industrial machines produce unique sounds based on CPU activity, hard drive movement, or even coil whine. Attackers can record these sounds and use AI to reconstruct passwords, encryption keys, and other sensitive data.

🔍 Examples of Sound-Based Attacks:

Keystroke Eavesdropping: AI can analyze typing sounds and reconstruct passwords.

CPU Noise Analysis: Different calculations produce different sound patterns, revealing cryptographic operations.

Fan Speed Variations: Some malware exploits this by encoding data in subtle fan speed changes.

💡 Example:

An attacker plants a hidden microphone near an operator's workstation and records keyboard sounds. Using AI, they accurately reconstruct the operator's login credentials. No hacking tools needed—just good ears.

Physical Recon: Breaking In Without Hacking

Sometimes, the best way to attack an industrial system isn't through a keyboard—it's through the front door. Physical reconnaissance is a critical part of any cyberattack, where attackers scout an industrial site for weak points.

🔍 Common Physical Security Failures:

Unattended workstations with unlocked sessions

Poorly secured server rooms (bad locks, no cameras)

Exposed USB ports and unpatched Ethernet jacks

Employees with no security awareness (social engineering goldmine)

💡 Example:

An attacker wearing a high-visibility vest and carrying a clipboard walks into a factory. No one questions them. They plug a Raspberry Pi into an open Ethernet jack, giving them remote access to the factory's network. Mission accomplished.

Real-World Side-Channel & Physical Recon Attacks

🔌 Case Study 1: The Power Grid Attack

In a real-world attack, researchers demonstrated that they could recover encryption keys from smart meters using power analysis. The attack was non-invasive, and within minutes, they extracted data that could be used to manipulate energy billing and control signals.

💀 Case Study 2: The Data Center Sound Attack

Researchers from Cambridge University used a smartphone to record CPU-generated noise from a laptop and successfully recovered the cryptographic keys. Imagine what could happen if someone did this in a factory or power plant.

🏃 Case Study 3: The Social Engineering Break-In

A security consultant (playing the role of an attacker) walked into a secured ICS facility with nothing but a fake ID badge. No one stopped him. He installed a rogue device on the network in under 10 minutes. The entire SCADA system was compromised—all because of bad physical security.

How to Defend Against These Attacks

If attackers can extract data just by listening, watching, or measuring signals, then traditional cybersecurity measures aren't enough. You need physical security and side-channel attack defenses too.

✅ **Use Shielding & Power Filters**: Prevent EM and power analysis attacks with Faraday cages and power filtering.
✅ **Encrypt Everything**: Even if an attacker intercepts data, make sure it's encrypted so they can't use it.
✅ **Randomize Processing & Power Consumption**: Use power-masking techniques to prevent predictable power leaks.
✅ **Monitor Physical Security**: Secure server rooms, control panels, and access points—and enforce strict visitor policies.
✅ **Train Employees**: Make sure employees recognize social engineering tricks and report suspicious activity.

Final Thoughts: Hackers Don't Always Need Code to Break In

Side-channel attacks and physical reconnaissance prove that hacking isn't always digital. Sometimes, it's about reading between the lines—or listening between the signals.

- Power analysis can steal encryption keys
- EM radiation can leak sensitive data
- Sound waves can expose passwords
- A poorly locked door can give an attacker all the access they need

The best hackers don't break in through firewalls—they walk in through open doors. Don't make it easy for them. ☺

4.5 Hardening IIoT Systems Against Unauthorized Discovery

The Hide-and-Seek Game You Can't Afford to Lose

If cybersecurity were a game, hackers would be world-class hide-and-seek champions—except they don't want to hide. They want to find everything you don't want them to, and trust me, they're really, really good at it. Exposed IIoT devices? Found. Open ports? Found. Weak passwords? Oh, definitely found.

Your job? Make their search as miserable as possible. Every industrial system has attack surfaces—entry points hackers use to sneak in and wreak havoc. From publicly exposed IIoT endpoints to weak SCADA authentication, the more an attacker can discover, the easier their job becomes. So, let's ruin their day.

This chapter is all about hardening IIoT systems against unauthorized discovery, making reconnaissance as painful as a Monday morning without coffee. Because if a hacker can't find your IIoT devices, they can't attack them.

Why IIoT Devices Are So Easy to Find

Before we start locking things down, let's answer a simple question: Why do hackers find IIoT devices so easily?

🔍 Because people leave them exposed.

Many IIoT and SCADA systems are publicly accessible on the internet. Tools like Shodan, Censys, and ZoomEye scan the internet 24/7, indexing every exposed industrial device like Google indexes websites. A quick search can reveal thousands of unprotected ICS systems, many still using default credentials.

🔍 Because manufacturers prioritize convenience over security.

Many industrial devices ship with open ports, default passwords, and unnecessary services enabled—all of which make setup easier but security worse. If admins don't change these settings, they're basically inviting attackers in.

🔍 Because people don't think like hackers.

Security teams focus on keeping attackers out—but hackers look for what's already exposed. That's why reconnaissance is the first stage of every cyberattack. If an attacker can map your network, fingerprint devices, and identify weak points, they're already halfway to breaking in.

So, how do we fix this? Let's start hiding.

Step 1: Reduce Your Attack Surface

The less visible your IIoT infrastructure is, the harder it is to attack. Here's how to make your systems disappear from an attacker's radar:

☐ **Block Public Exposure**

First rule of IIoT security: Your industrial devices should NEVER be directly accessible from the internet.

✅ Remove unnecessary public IP addresses.

✅ Use firewalls and VPNs to restrict access.

✅ Deploy network segmentation to isolate IIoT from corporate networks.

✅ Monitor your public-facing assets using tools like Shodan Monitor.

💡 **Example:**

A factory's SCADA system was accessible via the internet (big mistake). A hacker found it using Shodan, brute-forced the password (which was "admin123"), and took control of the entire system. The company's response? Disconnect the SCADA system from the internet—which should've been done from the start.

Step 2: Harden Your IIoT Devices

Even if a hacker finds your IIoT device, that doesn't mean they should be able to access or exploit it.

🔐 **Change Default Credentials (Immediately)**

IIoT manufacturers love shipping devices with default usernames and passwords (like "admin/admin"). Hackers know this, and they use automated scripts to brute-force weak logins.

✅ Change all default credentials before deployment.

✅ Use unique, strong passwords (or certificates) for every device.

✅ Implement multi-factor authentication (MFA) whenever possible.

💡 Example:

A hacker ran a brute-force attack on a factory's IIoT controller and guessed the password in seconds—because it was still the default. Lesson learned: Change the passwords. Always.

🔲 Disable Unnecessary Services

Many IIoT devices come with unnecessary services enabled by default, increasing attack surfaces.

✅ Disable Telnet, FTP, and other legacy services.

✅ Turn off debugging interfaces (like JTAG, UART) in production.

✅ Limit API access and use authentication tokens.

💡 Example:

A hacker exploited an open Telnet port on a water treatment plant's IIoT device, gaining full control. The fix? Disable Telnet and use SSH with key-based authentication.

🔲 Keep Firmware & Software Updated

Hackers love outdated firmware because it's full of known vulnerabilities.

✅ Regularly update all IIoT firmware and patches.

✅ Use automated patch management where possible.

✅ Remove unsupported legacy devices or put them behind secure gateways.

💡 Example:

A ransomware attack hit a power grid's IIoT controllers running unpatched firmware from 2015. The attack shut down operations for 48 hours. A single firmware update could have prevented the breach.

Step 3: Detect and Block Reconnaissance Attempts

Even with locked-down IIoT systems, attackers will still try to find ways in. Your job? Catch them in the act.

👀 Monitor for Unusual Scanning Activity

Attackers scan networks before launching attacks. Catching them early is crucial.

✅ Use intrusion detection systems (IDS) like Snort or Suricata.

✅ Deploy network monitoring tools (e.g., Zeek, Security Onion).

✅ Watch for repeated login failures, unexpected network probes, and unusual traffic patterns.

💡 Example:

A manufacturing plant's IDS detected multiple failed login attempts from an external IP. The IT team blocked the IP before an attack could occur.

🔲🔲 Implement Honeytokens and Honeypots

Fake IIoT devices can lure hackers into revealing themselves before they reach real systems.

✅ Deploy honeypots to trick attackers into attacking fake IIoT systems.

✅ Use honeytokens (fake credentials) to detect unauthorized access attempts.

✅ Monitor honeypot logs for signs of active reconnaissance.

💡 Example:

A security team set up a fake SCADA system as a honeypot. Within hours, attackers tried logging in with default credentials. The security team traced the attackers and blocked their access before real damage could be done.

Final Thoughts: Make Hackers Work for It

If hackers can't find your IIoT devices, they can't attack them. Your goal is to make discovery as painful as possible by:

✓ Removing public exposure (no internet-facing SCADA or IIoT devices!)

✓ Locking down device access (strong passwords, disabling unnecessary services)

✓ Monitoring for reconnaissance activity (catch hackers before they break in)

✓ Deploying deception strategies (honeypots, fake credentials)

Remember: Hackers are lazy. They go for easy targets. If your IIoT system is well-hidden and well-secured, they'll move on to someone else. Don't be the easy target. ☺

Chapter 5: Attacking and Exploiting Industrial IoT Devices

If you thought regular IoT was insecure, wait until you see what's lurking inside industrial IoT devices. From hardcoded credentials to firmware vulnerabilities, these systems are often so riddled with security gaps that hacking them feels like breaking into an unlocked house with a welcome mat that says 'Come On In!' Attackers know this, and they love nothing more than finding forgotten factory devices connected to the internet, just waiting to be exploited.

This chapter dives into the tactics, techniques, and procedures (TTPs) used to exploit IIoT devices, including firmware analysis, reverse engineering, and credential extraction. We'll explore real-world vulnerabilities, such as default passwords, insecure configurations, and supply chain risks, while also discussing best practices for secure firmware management and patching strategies.

5.1 Understanding IIoT Device Architectures and Firmware

The Anatomy of an IIoT Device: Not Just Another Smart Toaster

Let's be real—when most people hear "Internet of Things," they think of smart fridges that text you when you're out of milk or voice assistants that accidentally order 200 rolls of toilet paper. But Industrial IoT (IIoT) is a whole different beast. These devices don't just control your thermostat; they orchestrate power grids, manage factory automation, and keep water treatment plants running smoothly. If they go down, we're talking actual, real-world consequences—not just a warm beer in your fridge.

At their core, IIoT devices are a combination of embedded systems, sensors, actuators, communication modules, and firmware. Think of them like tiny computers with a very specific job—and a whole lot of security blind spots. In this chapter, we're tearing open the black box (metaphorically, unless you have a screwdriver handy) to understand what makes IIoT devices tick, how their firmware operates, and where security vulnerabilities lurk.

IIoT Device Architecture: What's Under the Hood?

An IIoT device isn't just a sensor glued to a network. It's a complex, multi-layered system with several key components:

1️ Hardware Layer (The Brains and Brawn)

At the heart of every IIoT device is an embedded system—a specialized computing unit designed for a specific function. The hardware usually consists of:

Microcontrollers (MCUs) and Processors (MPUs): These execute the device's software. Some use ARM Cortex-M chips (low power, simple tasks), while others run on x86 or RISC-V architectures.

Memory (Flash, EEPROM, RAM): Flash stores firmware, RAM helps with execution, and EEPROM holds persistent settings.

Sensors and Actuators: Sensors collect data (temperature, pressure, motion), while actuators take action (opening valves, shutting down machinery).

Communication Interfaces: IIoT devices talk to each other and to control systems using protocols like UART, SPI, I2C, CAN bus, or Ethernet.

2️ Firmware Layer (The Invisible Conductor)

Firmware is the low-level software running on an IIoT device. Unlike traditional software, firmware is burned into the device (often on Flash memory) and controls how the hardware interacts with the outside world. It consists of:

Bootloader: The first thing that runs when a device powers on. It checks the integrity of the firmware and loads the main application.

Real-Time Operating System (RTOS) or Bare Metal Code: Some IIoT devices run lightweight RTOSs like FreeRTOS or VxWorks, while others operate without an OS using direct firmware control.

Device Drivers: These act as translators between firmware and hardware components.

Network Stack: Enables communication using TCP/IP, MQTT, Modbus, OPC-UA, and other protocols.

3️⃣ Connectivity Layer (The Nervous System)

IIoT devices aren't standalone—they need to send and receive data in real time. The connectivity layer includes:

Wired Interfaces: Ethernet, CAN bus, RS-485 (used in industrial settings).

Wireless Technologies: Wi-Fi, Zigbee, LoRaWAN, NB-IoT, 5G (each with its own security trade-offs).

Cloud & Edge Computing Integration: Many IIoT devices transmit data to cloud platforms (AWS IoT, Azure IoT Hub, Google Cloud IoT) or process it locally at the edge.

4️⃣ Application Layer (The Decision-Maker)

This is where the real data processing, analytics, and automation logic happen. It can be:

On the device itself (Edge AI, ML inference models).

On a gateway (intermediate device aggregating data from multiple IIoT endpoints).

In the cloud (centralized control, analytics, dashboards).

Firmware: The Lifeblood of IIoT Security (and Attackers' Favorite Playground)

Firmware is what makes an IIoT device function—and unfortunately, what often makes it vulnerable. Unlike regular software, firmware isn't frequently updated (sometimes never), meaning bugs and security holes stick around for years.

● Common Firmware Security Risks

1️⃣ Hardcoded Credentials:

Manufacturers often bake default usernames and passwords into firmware—and attackers know exactly where to find them.

Example: The infamous Mirai botnet exploited hardcoded credentials in IoT devices to launch DDoS attacks.

2️⃣ Unencrypted Firmware Updates:

If firmware updates aren't signed and encrypted, attackers can inject malicious code into an update package.

Example: Attackers exploited weak update mechanisms in industrial routers to deploy backdoor access.

3️⃣ Insecure Bootloaders:

A poorly secured bootloader lets attackers modify firmware at startup, allowing persistent malware infections.

Some devices lack Secure Boot, meaning malicious firmware can be flashed without resistance.

4️⃣ Buffer Overflows & Memory Corruption:

Many IIoT devices use C/C++ code, which lacks memory safety, making them vulnerable to buffer overflow attacks.

Attackers can overwrite memory regions, hijack execution flow, and take control of the device.

5️⃣ No Secure Firmware Update Mechanism:

Many IIoT devices lack over-the-air (OTA) update capabilities, meaning firmware updates require manual intervention—which rarely happens in industrial environments.

Securing IIoT Architectures and Firmware: How Not to Get Hacked

So, how do we keep IIoT devices from becoming hacker playgrounds? Here's a checklist for securing both architecture and firmware:

✅ **Implement Secure Boot**: Prevent unauthorized firmware modifications.
✅ **Use Code Signing & Firmware Encryption**: Ensure only authentic firmware runs on devices.

✅ **Enforce Strong Access Controls**: No default credentials—use unique passwords and multi-factor authentication (MFA).

✅ **Harden Communication Protocols**: Encrypt all network traffic (TLS, VPNs, IPsec).

✅ **Regularly Update Firmware**: Patch vulnerabilities before attackers exploit them.

✅ **Implement Secure OTA Updates**: Ensure updates are cryptographically signed and verified.

✅ **Use Hardware Security Modules (HSMs):** Secure cryptographic operations and key storage.

Final Thoughts: If It's Smart, It's Hackable

IIoT devices aren't just "dumb" sensors—they're powerful, complex, and often insecure. Hackers love them because they're often forgotten, unpatched, and exposed to the internet.

If you take one thing from this chapter, let it be this: Never trust an IIoT device out of the box. If it ships with default passwords, weak firmware, or open ports, it's just waiting to be hacked. Secure it before someone else does. 😼

5.2 Exploiting Hardcoded Credentials in Industrial Devices

Hardcoded Credentials: The Skeleton Key to IIoT Systems

Picture this: You buy a new smart factory robot, unbox it, and—out of pure curiosity—you check the default login credentials in the manual. It's something absurdly simple like admin/admin or root/root. You think, "There's no way they left it like this, right?" So you log in… and boom, full access. No security prompts, no password change requirement—just an open door waiting for someone to walk in.

Now imagine that hundreds of thousands of industrial IoT (IIoT) devices are deployed with these same hardcoded credentials, and companies forget to change them. Hackers know this all too well, and it's one of the most common (and embarrassingly easy) ways to breach industrial systems.

So in this chapter, we're diving deep into why manufacturers still hardcode credentials, how attackers exploit them, and most importantly, how to secure IIoT devices before they become an entry point for cyberattacks.

What Are Hardcoded Credentials and Why Do They Exist?

Hardcoded credentials are pre-set usernames and passwords embedded directly into device firmware. They exist for one simple reason: convenience for manufacturers and engineers.

Common Reasons for Hardcoded Credentials:

1☐ **Ease of Deployment**: Engineers and technicians need quick access during setup and maintenance. Instead of generating unique credentials, manufacturers bake in a universal username and password.

2☐ **Remote Support**: Vendors might use hardcoded credentials for remote troubleshooting, allowing them to log in without asking for credentials each time.

3☐ **Legacy Systems & Compatibility**: Some old-school industrial systems were never designed for individual user authentication, so they rely on one global login.

4☐ **Laziness & Poor Security Culture**: Let's be real—sometimes it's just bad security practices that no one bothered to fix.

Examples of Hardcoded Credentials in the Wild

Mirai Botnet (2016): The infamous Mirai malware scanned the internet for IoT devices using default passwords, hijacking them into a botnet that launched massive DDoS attacks.

SCADA Vendor Backdoors: Some industrial control system (ICS) vendors left undocumented "support" accounts in their firmware—accounts that attackers eventually found and exploited.

VoIP & Industrial Routers: Many industrial networking devices have been compromised using default logins like 'admin' or '1234', leading to network takeovers.

How Attackers Exploit Hardcoded Credentials

A hacker's workflow for exploiting hardcoded credentials is painfully simple. If it's online, it's fair game.

Step 1: Scanning for Vulnerable Devices

Attackers use search engines like Shodan, Censys, and ZoomEye to locate internet-exposed IIoT devices. These tools allow them to filter devices by:

Manufacturer and model

Open ports (e.g., 23 for Telnet, 22 for SSH, 80 for HTTP login pages)

Protocol type (Modbus, DNP3, MQTT, etc.)

For example, a simple Shodan query like:

port:23 "SCADA"

could reveal thousands of unprotected industrial systems with open Telnet access.

Step 2: Checking Public Lists of Default Credentials

Many manufacturers reuse the same default credentials across devices. Attackers check resources like:

Default password lists (available in cybersecurity repositories and hacker forums)

Vendor manuals (which often list default logins in plain text)

Past data breaches (credential leaks from previous hacks)

For example, a quick Google search for:

default password site:vendor.com

often leads to official documentation listing factory-set logins.

Step 3: Logging in and Taking Over the Device

Once an attacker has the credentials, they simply:

Log in via Telnet, SSH, HTTP, or an API interface.

Disable security features (firewalls, logging, alerts).

Install malware, change configurations, or create a backdoor.

From here, the attacker can:

Pivot into the industrial network to access more critical systems.

Turn off safety controls (which can lead to physical damage in factories).

Deploy ransomware or botnets (holding critical infrastructure hostage).

Case Study: The Mirai Botnet & Industrial IoT Attacks

The Mirai botnet attack in 2016 was a wake-up call for IIoT security. The malware scanned the internet for devices using default credentials, logged in, and converted them into zombie bots.

This botnet:

Took down major websites and infrastructure using massive DDoS attacks.

Infected hundreds of thousands of IoT and IIoT devices, including industrial routers and CCTV systems.

Exploited weak, hardcoded passwords that manufacturers never removed.

The scariest part? Mirai's source code was leaked, meaning any hacker can modify and redeploy it on new vulnerable IIoT devices.

Defending Against Hardcoded Credential Exploits

So, how do we stop attackers from walking through the front door? Here's what every industrial security team should do ASAP.

✓ 1. Change Default Credentials Immediately

Step 1: Inventory all IIoT devices.

Step 2: Locate any using default usernames and passwords.

Step 3: Change them to strong, unique passwords.

If a device doesn't allow you to change credentials, consider replacing it (or putting it behind a firewall).

✅ 2. Disable Unnecessary Remote Access

Block Telnet (port 23) and SSH (port 22) if not needed.

Use VPNs or secure gateways for remote connections instead of exposing devices online.

Implement network segmentation to keep IIoT systems isolated from IT networks.

✅ 3. Enforce Multi-Factor Authentication (MFA)

If possible, require MFA for administrator logins.

Use hardware security keys or one-time passcodes (OTP) for critical systems.

✅ 4. Implement Network Monitoring and Alerts

Set up SIEM (Security Information and Event Management) tools to detect unauthorized logins.

Use honeytokens (fake credentials) to alert on credential theft attempts.

✅ 5. Push Manufacturers for Secure Defaults

Ask vendors to remove hardcoded credentials in future firmware updates.

Use devices that support unique, randomized passwords out of the box.

Advocate for secure-by-design principles in IIoT product development.

Final Thoughts: Don't Let Your IIoT Devices Have the Same Password as Your Luggage

Leaving hardcoded credentials in an IIoT device is like leaving your house key under the doormat—with a neon sign that says "FREE ENTRY." Attackers don't need sophisticated zero-day exploits when they can just Google a manufacturer's manual and log in like a regular user.

So, if you're managing an IIoT network, audit your devices now. If you find hardcoded credentials, change them, lock them down, and pressure vendors to do better. Because in industrial cybersecurity, the easiest exploit is always the first one hackers will try.

5.3 Reverse Engineering and Tampering with ICS Firmware

Cracking Open the Industrial Vault

Imagine you just bought a brand-new industrial controller, a sleek little device that helps run an entire factory. But instead of plugging it in like a responsible engineer, you do what any curious hacker would do—you grab a screwdriver, pop it open, and start poking around its firmware.

Congratulations! You've just stepped into the world of reverse engineering—where we dissect industrial control system (ICS) firmware to understand how it works, find vulnerabilities, and, if we're feeling mischievous (or just security-conscious), figure out how an attacker might tamper with it.

Why does this matter? Because ICS firmware is the brain of industrial systems, controlling everything from power grids to water treatment plants. If an attacker can modify that firmware, they can inject malware, disable safety mechanisms, or even cause physical damage to industrial infrastructure.

So, in this chapter, we're diving deep into:

✓ How ICS firmware works and why it's a juicy target for hackers.

✓ The tools and techniques used to reverse engineer industrial firmware.

✓ How attackers modify and deploy malicious firmware.

✓ Most importantly—how to defend against firmware tampering attacks.

Grab your JTAG debugger and some coffee—we're cracking some firmware!

What Is ICS Firmware and Why Is It a Target?

Firmware is the low-level software embedded into ICS devices like programmable logic controllers (PLCs), remote terminal units (RTUs), and industrial sensors. Unlike traditional software, firmware is stored on read-only memory (ROM), flash memory, or EEPROMs, making it resistant to modifications—but not immune.

Why Do Attackers Love ICS Firmware?

1⬜ **Total Device Control**: If an attacker modifies firmware, they can take full control of an industrial device—overriding safety settings, issuing fake commands, or creating backdoors.

2⬜ **Persistence**: Unlike regular malware that gets wiped after a reboot, firmware-level malware survives resets and even OS reinstallation.

3⬜ **Harder to Detect**: Traditional antivirus and security tools don't scan firmware, making it a stealthy attack vector.

4⬜ **Supply Chain Attacks**: If an attacker compromises firmware before the device is shipped, they can distribute backdoored ICS devices worldwide.

Case in point? Stuxnet. This legendary worm targeted Siemens PLCs, modifying their firmware to send false safety signals while secretly sabotaging uranium enrichment centrifuges. This wasn't just hacking—this was cyber warfare at the firmware level.

Reverse Engineering ICS Firmware: Tools & Techniques

Reverse engineering is like hacking time-traveling VHS tapes—except instead of figuring out how to fix an old movie, we're breaking down industrial firmware to see how it ticks.

Here's how security researchers (and hackers) do it:

Step 1: Extracting the Firmware

To analyze firmware, you first need to get your hands on it. Attackers typically extract firmware using:

Manufacturer Websites: Some vendors post firmware updates online, which attackers can download and analyze.

Physical Extraction: Using hardware tools like JTAG, SPI, or UART debuggers to pull firmware directly from a device's flash memory.

Network Sniffing: Intercepting firmware updates sent over unencrypted network protocols (shoutout to manufacturers still using plain HTTP ☐).

Step 2: Analyzing the Firmware Binary

Once extracted, firmware needs to be dissected and understood. This is where reverse engineering tools come into play:

◆ **Binwalk**: The Swiss Army knife of firmware analysis, used to unpack and analyze embedded files.

◆ **Ghidra & IDA Pro**: Disassemblers that turn binary code into human-readable assembly instructions.

◆ **Radare2**: An open-source reverse engineering framework for analyzing firmware structure.

◆ **Firmware-Mod-Kit**: A toolset for modifying and repacking firmware images.

A quick Binwalk scan might reveal a treasure trove of files:

$ binwalk -e industrial_firmware.bin

```
DECIMAL   HEX       DESCRIPTION
----------------------------------------------------------------
1024      0x400     gzip compressed data, from Unix
2048      0x800     ELF executable, MIPS architecture
4096      0x1000    Linux filesystem (SquashFS)
```

This tells us the firmware contains a Linux-based OS (common in ICS devices), an executable binary, and some compressed files. Now we dig deeper.

Tampering with ICS Firmware: Attack Scenarios

Once an attacker understands how a firmware image works, they can modify it for malicious purposes. Here are some real-world firmware tampering techniques:

1☐ Injecting Backdoors

Attackers can modify firmware to add hidden admin accounts, enabling persistent access even after reboots.

Example:

Modify /etc/passwd to insert a new admin user with root access.

Patch the firmware's SSH daemon to accept a hacker's SSH key by default.

2️ Disabling Security Features

Modify firmware to turn off logging, making attacks harder to detect.

Patch firmware to disable firmware integrity checks, allowing attackers to install future malicious updates.

3️ Firmware-Based Ransomware

Encrypt critical industrial functions at the firmware level, demanding ransom for recovery.

Lock operators out of ICS control panels, disrupting entire factory operations.

Defending Against Firmware Tampering Attacks

So how do we prevent attackers from hijacking ICS firmware? Here are the best defense strategies:

✅ 1. Implement Secure Boot

Ensure ICS devices use cryptographic signatures to verify firmware authenticity before booting.

If modified firmware is detected, the device should refuse to load it.

✅ 2. Encrypt Firmware Updates

Always use digitally signed and encrypted firmware updates.

Disable rollback attacks by preventing older, vulnerable firmware from being reinstalled.

✅ 3. Restrict Physical Access

Disable JTAG, UART, and other debugging interfaces unless explicitly needed.

Implement tamper-evident hardware enclosures to prevent physical attacks.

✅ 4. Monitor Firmware Integrity

Use firmware whitelisting to detect unauthorized modifications.

Regularly scan ICS devices for unexpected firmware changes.

✅ 5. Push Vendors for Secure-by-Design Firmware

Demand manufacturers remove hardcoded backdoors from factory firmware.

Advocate for regular security patches and firmware updates.

Final Thoughts: If You Can Hack It, So Can Someone Else

Reverse engineering ICS firmware is like unlocking a hidden level in an industrial security game—except the stakes are real factories, power plants, and critical infrastructure. Attackers who gain control over firmware don't just steal data—they can shut down production lines, sabotage industrial processes, or worse, cause catastrophic physical damage.

So whether you're an ICS security pro, an ethical hacker, or just someone who enjoys dissecting firmware over coffee, remember: if you don't test your firmware's security, attackers will gladly do it for you.

5.4 Weaponizing Malware and Ransomware Against IIoT Systems

Malware in IIoT: When Your Factory Gets a Virus

Imagine walking into your smart factory on a Monday morning, coffee in hand, expecting a smooth day of industrial automation. But instead of humming machinery and synchronized robotic arms, you see a giant red message on every control screen:

💀 "Your SCADA system has been encrypted! Pay 100 BTC to restore operations!" 💀

At this point, two thoughts cross your mind:

"Oh no, the factory is dead."

"Wait, Bitcoin prices just went up… this ransom is ridiculous!"

Welcome to the world of IIoT ransomware, where cybercriminals don't just steal data—they hold entire industrial operations hostage. And if you thought traditional malware was bad, IIoT malware can cause actual physical destruction, turning smart factories, power grids, and water treatment plants into cyber-chaos zones.

So, in this chapter, we're diving into:

✅ The types of malware targeting IIoT and SCADA systems.

✅ How attackers deploy ransomware against industrial networks.

✅ Real-world attacks that shook the industrial world.

✅ Most importantly—how to fight back and protect your systems.

Buckle up. We're about to take a wild ride into the dark side of industrial hacking.

The Evolution of IIoT Malware: From Annoying to Destructive

Malware has been around for decades, but IIoT-focused malware is a different beast. Instead of just stealing passwords or crashing computers, these cyber weapons can shut down manufacturing plants, blow up industrial equipment, and disrupt entire supply chains.

Here's a breakdown of major malware types that target IIoT:

1️ Traditional Malware: Old Dogs, New Tricks

Even old-school malware like Trojans and worms can wreak havoc on industrial systems. If a simple keylogger gets into an engineering workstation, attackers can steal SCADA login credentials and remotely control industrial processes.

☑ **Example**: The Havex Trojan targeted energy companies, using remote access trojans (RATs) to spy on ICS networks.

2️⃣ ICS-Specific Malware: Designed for Destruction

Attackers are now crafting malware specifically designed for IIoT and SCADA environments.

☑ **Example**: Stuxnet (2010) was the world's first cyber weapon, infecting Siemens PLCs to sabotage Iran's nuclear centrifuges. It didn't just steal data—it physically destroyed industrial machines by altering their firmware.

☑ **Example**: Triton/Trisis (2017) targeted safety instrumented systems (SIS) in oil refineries, attempting to disable emergency shutdown mechanisms. That's next-level cyber-physical sabotage.

3️⃣ Ransomware: Pay Up or Shut Down

Ransomware has evolved from encrypting files to locking down entire industrial networks. Unlike regular ransomware, IIoT ransomware goes after production environments, forcing factories and infrastructure to grind to a halt.

☑ **Example**: EKANS Ransomware (2020) specifically targeted ICS networks, shutting down industrial control systems by terminating crucial processes.

☑ **Example**: Colonial Pipeline Attack (2021) wasn't even ICS-specific ransomware, but by infecting corporate IT systems, it caused an entire fuel pipeline shutdown across the U.S.

The message is clear: IIoT is a prime target for malware, and the stakes are real.

How Attackers Deploy Malware & Ransomware in IIoT

◆ 1. Supply Chain Attacks

If attackers can compromise a trusted vendor's software, they can infect thousands of IIoT devices before they even leave the factory.

✅ **Example**: SolarWinds Attack (2020) injected malware into a routine software update, infecting government agencies and corporations worldwide.

◆ 2. Exploiting Unpatched Vulnerabilities

Many IIoT systems still run outdated firmware and unpatched software, making them an easy target for malware.

✅ **Example**: EternalBlue Exploit (used in the WannaCry ransomware attack) leveraged a Microsoft Windows flaw to spread across networks in minutes.

◆ 3. Phishing and Social Engineering

Attackers often trick employees into clicking malicious links or plugging in infected USB drives.

✅ **Example**: Ukrainian Power Grid Attack (2015) started with a simple phishing email. The malware used remote access to shut down power to 230,000 people.

◆ 4. Exploiting Remote Access & VPNs

IIoT devices are often remotely accessible via weakly protected VPNs or RDP sessions. If an attacker gets in, it's game over.

✅ **Example**: The Colonial Pipeline attackers used a single stolen password to access the network via VPN—no multi-factor authentication required.

How to Defend Against IIoT Malware & Ransomware

So, how do we fight back against these threats? Here's a battle-tested security strategy to keep your IIoT systems safe.

✅ 1. Implement Network Segmentation (Don't Let Malware Spread!)

Separate IT and OT networks to prevent ransomware from moving between them.

Use firewalls and DMZs to limit access between corporate and industrial environments.

✅ 2. Patch & Update Everything (Yes, Even Legacy Systems)

Regularly update ICS firmware and software to patch known vulnerabilities.

If a system can't be patched, implement compensating controls like network monitoring.

✅ 3. Enable Multi-Factor Authentication (No More Easy Logins!)

Require MFA for all remote access, especially for VPNs and engineering workstations.

Disable default passwords and unused accounts on IIoT devices.

✅ 4. Implement Endpoint Detection & Response (EDR)

Deploy EDR solutions that can detect malware execution and suspicious behaviors on IIoT systems.

Monitor for unexpected process terminations, a key sign of ICS-targeting ransomware.

✅ 5. Prepare for the Worst: Backup & Incident Response

Keep offline backups of all critical IIoT configurations.

Have a tested incident response plan that includes ransomware containment and recovery.

Final Thoughts: Your Factory vs. The Hackers

At this point, you might be thinking, "Wow, securing IIoT is like defending a castle against an army of cybercriminals."

Well, you're not wrong. Hackers are constantly evolving their attacks, and IIoT systems present a massive attack surface that's hard to defend.

But here's the good news: attackers rely on lazy security. They thrive on default passwords, unpatched firmware, and exposed IIoT devices. If you follow the security measures we just covered, you'll make their job much harder—and your smart factory much safer.

So next time you see a ransomware attack on the news, take a deep breath and think:

"Not my factory, not today." 💪

5.5 Implementing Secure Firmware and Patch Management Policies

Why Updating Firmware is Like Eating Vegetables (You Hate It, But It's Necessary)

Let's be honest—nobody wakes up excited about firmware updates. Updating industrial systems is like eating vegetables: we know it's good for us, but we avoid it until something forces our hand (like a ransomware attack or an auditor breathing down our necks).

Yet, skipping firmware updates is one of the fastest ways to turn your industrial network into a hacker's playground. Attackers love outdated firmware because it's filled with security flaws that vendors have already fixed—but you haven't applied yet.

Remember Stuxnet? That famous malware didn't break into Iran's nuclear program by brute force. Nope. It exploited unpatched vulnerabilities in Siemens PLCs. And if a nation-state attack sounds too extreme, consider this:

80% of ICS vulnerabilities reported in the last five years were due to outdated software and firmware.

Many IIoT devices are still running firmware from over a decade ago—because "if it ain't broke, don't fix it" is the unofficial motto of industrial security.

Hackers don't need fancy zero-day exploits when they can just target known vulnerabilities with publicly available exploit code.

So, let's talk about how to actually implement a secure firmware and patch management strategy that doesn't leave your factory vulnerable to cyberattacks.

Why Firmware Updates Matter (and Why People Avoid Them)

1⃣ Why It Matters: Firmware Controls Everything

Firmware is the low-level software that controls everything in industrial IoT (IIoT), SCADA, and OT environments. It's embedded in:

✅ PLCs (Programmable Logic Controllers)

✅ RTUs (Remote Terminal Units)

✅ Smart sensors

✅ Industrial gateways

✅ HMI systems

If your firmware is compromised, attackers can hijack your entire industrial process—manipulating machines, shutting down production, or even causing physical damage.

2️⃣ Why People Avoid It: "If We Update, It Might Break!"

Unlike IT environments, where updating software is a routine task, industrial updates come with real risks:

❌ **Downtime**: Updating firmware might require shutting down critical systems, costing millions in lost production.
❌ **Compatibility Issues**: Some updates break integrations with legacy hardware.
❌ **Lack of Vendor Support**: Some devices never receive updates because the vendor abandoned the product.

So, how do we balance security with operational reliability? Let's break it down.

How to Implement a Secure Firmware and Patch Management Policy

◆ 1. Asset Inventory: Know What You're Running

You can't secure what you don't know exists. Start by creating an inventory of all devices running firmware in your industrial network.

✅ **Document everything**: Device model, firmware version, last update date, and vendor support status.
✅ **Identify end-of-life devices**: If a device no longer receives updates, it's a security risk. Plan for replacements or compensating security measures.

✓ **Monitor for new vulnerabilities**: Subscribe to vendor security bulletins, ICS-CERT alerts, and CVE databases.

◆ 2. Establish a Firmware Update Schedule

Instead of waiting for a crisis, implement scheduled firmware updates with minimal disruption.

✓ **Quarterly or Bi-Annual Updates**: Plan updates during scheduled maintenance windows.

✓ **Emergency Patching**: If a critical vulnerability is discovered, have a process for expedited patching without waiting for the next scheduled update.

✓ **Test Before Deployment**: Use a sandbox environment to test updates before applying them to production systems.

◆ 3. Implement a Risk-Based Patching Strategy

Not all updates are equal. Some are critical, others can wait.

🔥 Immediate Patch (High Risk)

Vulnerabilities with public exploits available (i.e., Metasploit module exists).

Issues that allow remote code execution or complete system takeover.

Devices connected to public-facing networks.

⚠️ Scheduled Update (Medium Risk)

Vulnerabilities that require local access to exploit.

Updates that improve security but aren't urgent.

☐ Low Priority / Monitor (Low Risk)

Minor bug fixes with no security impact.

Devices in air-gapped networks with strict access controls.

◆ 4. Secure the Update Process (No, Don't Just Download from Google)

Updating firmware isn't as simple as downloading and clicking "Install." Attackers often use fake firmware updates to inject malware into IIoT systems.

✅ **Verify update sources**: Always download from official vendor portals. Never use third-party links.

✅ **Check digital signatures**: Ensure firmware updates are cryptographically signed by the vendor.

✅ **Use a secure update mechanism**: If possible, use trusted firmware update protocols (like TLS-encrypted OTA updates).

✅ **Restrict update permissions**: Only authorized personnel should be able to upload new firmware.

◆ 5. Implement Rollback Mechanisms (Because Things Can Go Wrong)

Ever installed an update, only to find out it broke everything? Now imagine that happening in a nuclear power plant or a water treatment facility.

✅ Backup configurations before updating.

✅ Test updates on a small subset of devices before rolling out system-wide.

✅ Have a rollback plan in case an update causes failures.

Real-World Attacks That Could Have Been Prevented with Firmware Updates

✳ Stuxnet (2010)

Exploited unpatched vulnerabilities in Siemens PLCs.

Used USB malware to spread through air-gapped networks.

Lesson: If firmware updates had been applied, Stuxnet's attack would have been much harder to pull off.

✳ EKANS Ransomware (2020)

Targeted ICS systems by shutting down critical processes.

Exploited unpatched vulnerabilities in industrial software.

Lesson: Regular firmware and patch management could have reduced attack impact.

Final Thoughts: Patch or Get Pwned

Here's the harsh truth: if you don't patch, you're already compromised.

Attackers don't need zero-day exploits when they can just Google known vulnerabilities in outdated firmware. Keeping firmware updated is one of the simplest and most effective ways to secure IIoT environments.

Sure, updates can be inconvenient, but so is having your entire smart factory shut down by ransomware. So next time someone says "We don't have time to update firmware", remind them:

- You don't have time for a cyberattack either.
- Hackers love outdated firmware—don't make their job easy.
- Patching today is cheaper than recovering from an attack tomorrow.

So eat your vegetables, update your firmware, and keep your IIoT systems secure. Because no one wants to be the next Stuxnet victim. 🚀

Chapter 6: Wireless and RF Security in Industrial IoT

Wireless tech in IIoT is like that one coworker who's both essential and a security nightmare. Zigbee, LoRa, LPWAN, 5G, RFID—these protocols keep smart factories running, but they also open up a buffet of hacking opportunities. If an attacker can sniff, jam, or spoof wireless communications, they can disrupt entire industrial operations without ever stepping foot inside the building.

This chapter examines the security challenges of wireless communications in IIoT environments, covering common wireless protocols, attack vectors, and real-world exploitation techniques. We'll explore methods like RF sniffing, jamming, replay attacks, and man-in-the-middle interception, as well as defensive strategies to harden IIoT wireless communications against cyber threats.

6.1 Common Wireless Protocols in IIoT: Zigbee, LoRa, LPWAN, 5G

Wireless Chaos: How Industrial IoT Talks Without Wires (and Sometimes Without Security)

Picture this: You walk into a smart factory, and it looks like something straight out of a sci-fi movie. Machines hum, robotic arms move with precision, sensors track everything from temperature to vibrations, and not a single wire in sight. Everything is wireless—because in the modern Industrial IoT (IIoT) world, cables are as outdated as dial-up internet.

But here's the problem—wireless tech is both a blessing and a security nightmare.

Wireless IIoT communication is like an open-air concert: anyone with the right equipment can listen in, jam the signals, or even fake being part of the system. Attackers don't need physical access to your factory; they just need an antenna, some basic hacking tools, and a bit of patience.

Before we dive into how to secure these wireless protocols, let's get a grip on how they work.

The Wireless Foundations of Industrial IoT

Industrial IoT relies on low-power, long-range, and high-efficiency wireless protocols to connect sensors, controllers, and monitoring systems. The right protocol depends on the use case—do you need high speed? Low power? Massive coverage?

Here are the four big players:

Protocol	Best For	Pros	Cons
Zigbee	Smart sensors, automation	Low power, mesh networking	Short range, interference
LoRa (Long Range)	Long-distance sensors	Huge coverage, low power	Low data rates
LPWAN (Low-Power Wide-Area Networks)	Remote monitoring	Covers massive areas, good battery life	Latency issues
5G	High-speed industrial automation	Ultra-fast, low latency	Expensive, power-hungry

Let's break them down one by one.

◆ Zigbee: The King of Short-Range Industrial Automation

If you've ever played with a smart home device, chances are it was running on Zigbee. But Zigbee isn't just for your smart lights—it's a staple in IIoT networks, especially for factories and smart grids.

✅ How It Works:

Zigbee creates a low-power, low-speed mesh network.

Devices talk to each other and form a self-healing network (if one device fails, others reroute the data).

It runs on 2.4 GHz (same as Wi-Fi), making it easy to deploy but also prone to interference.

⚠️ Security Concerns:

Weak encryption: Older Zigbee versions used no encryption at all.

Default keys: Many devices ship with hardcoded encryption keys, making them easy to crack.

Jamming attacks: Since it operates on 2.4 GHz, Wi-Fi interference or a cheap jammer can bring down Zigbee networks.

🔒 How to Secure It:

✓ Always use Zigbee 3.0, which has stronger encryption.

✓ Change default security keys (don't assume the vendor did it for you).

✓ Use network segmentation to keep Zigbee devices isolated from critical systems.

◆ LoRa (Long Range): The Master of Remote Industrial Sensors

Let's say you have sensors spread over an entire oil field or covering miles of a power grid—you can't rely on Wi-Fi or cellular networks. That's where LoRa (Long Range) comes in.

✅ How It Works:

Uses sub-GHz frequencies (915 MHz in the US) for ultra-long-range communication.

Devices can send data up to 10 miles away with minimal power consumption.

It's great for battery-powered IIoT devices that only need to send small amounts of data.

⚠️ Security Concerns:

LoRa networks are easy to sniff—attackers can eavesdrop on signals from miles away.

No built-in encryption (unless configured manually).

Replay attacks—an attacker can capture LoRa signals and rebroadcast them to manipulate data.

🔒 How to Secure It:

✓ Always enable AES-128 encryption at the device and gateway level.

✓ Use rolling encryption keys to prevent replay attacks.

✓ Implement whitelisting so only authorized devices can communicate.

◆ LPWAN: The Backbone of Low-Power Industrial IoT

LPWAN (Low-Power Wide-Area Networks) is a broad category of long-range, low-power wireless networks. LoRa is a type of LPWAN, but others include Sigfox and NB-IoT.

✅ How It Works:

Designed for massive IoT deployments (smart cities, industrial monitoring).

Supports millions of devices over vast areas.

Low bandwidth but extreme power efficiency (battery life can last 10+ years).

⚠️ Security Concerns:

Most LPWAN protocols don't encrypt data by default.

Lack of authentication—an attacker can spoof a device and inject false data.

Signal jamming is a serious risk because LPWAN networks operate on unlicensed frequencies.

🔒 How to Secure It:

✓ Use end-to-end encryption at the application layer.

✓ Implement strong device authentication before allowing communication.

✓ Monitor for sudden spikes in traffic, which could indicate an attack.

◆ 5G: The Speed Demon of Industrial IoT

If LoRa is like sending postcards, 5G is like fiber-optic internet on steroids. 5G isn't just about faster smartphones—it's also revolutionizing industrial automation.

✅ How It Works:

Provides blazing-fast speeds (up to 10 Gbps) and ultra-low latency (<1 ms).

Supports millions of IIoT devices per square mile.

Enables real-time AI-driven automation in smart factories.

⚠️ Security Concerns:

5G networks rely on cloud infrastructure, increasing attack surfaces.

Supply chain risks—if your 5G equipment comes from a compromised vendor, your entire factory could be at risk.

DDoS risks—5G allows massive device connectivity, which means botnet attacks can scale exponentially.

🔒 How to Secure It:

✓ Use private 5G networks for critical infrastructure.

✓ Implement Zero Trust security—don't assume any device is safe.

✓ Continuously monitor anomalous traffic that could indicate a cyberattack.

Final Thoughts: Choose Wisely, Secure Aggressively

Wireless makes IIoT smarter, faster, and more efficient, but it also introduces security risks that attackers love to exploit. Whether you're using Zigbee for factory automation, LoRa for remote sensors, LPWAN for smart grids, or 5G for high-speed robotics, you must secure your wireless networks.

Because let's face it—if an attacker can sit outside your facility with a cheap antenna and break into your industrial systems...well, you might as well have left the front door open.

So, choose your protocols wisely, lock them down tightly, and always assume someone's trying to hack you. 🚀

6.2 Sniffing and Intercepting Wireless IIoT Traffic Using SDR

Hackers with Radios: The Unseen Threat in IIoT

Let me tell you a story. A guy in a hoodie (because hackers always wear hoodies, right?) sits in his car outside a factory. He's not breaking in through the front gate. Nope. He's got a software-defined radio (SDR) plugged into his laptop, and he's listening to everything your factory's wireless devices are saying. Sensors, controllers, industrial robots—if they're sending signals over the air without proper encryption, he can eavesdrop, record, and even manipulate them.

Sound far-fetched? It's not.

Hackers, security researchers, and curious hobbyists have been using SDR for years to sniff and intercept unprotected wireless communications. And industrial IoT systems, with their legacy protocols and weak encryption, are prime targets. If your factory is using Zigbee, LoRa, LPWAN, or even RFID/NFC, it's time to pay attention—because attackers already are.

What is SDR, and Why Should You Worry?

A software-defined radio (SDR) is a radio communication system where components that were traditionally hardware-based (like tuners and demodulators) are implemented via software. In simple terms, an SDR can listen, capture, and even modify wireless signals across a huge range of frequencies.

Why SDR is a Game Changer for Hackers (and Security Pros)

✅ Can scan and capture signals from multiple IIoT devices at once

✅ Works with cheap USB devices like RTL-SDR ($30 on Amazon!)

✅ Can replay or modify intercepted data to inject malicious commands

✅ Bypasses physical security—attackers don't need direct access to your systems

If that doesn't scare you yet, let's talk about real-world attacks.

How Attackers Use SDR to Intercept IIoT Traffic

1️⃣ Passive Eavesdropping (Just Listening to Your Factory Talk)

Think of wireless IIoT like people talking loudly in a crowded room. If your communications aren't encrypted, anyone with an SDR can listen in and capture sensitive information.

✅ Example:

A hacker outside your factory uses RTL-SDR to sniff unsecured Zigbee or LoRa communications. He logs data from sensors and control systems, mapping your factory's entire network—no hacking tools required, just a radio receiver.

💀 The Risk:

Attackers can extract sensitive data like machine statuses, production schedules, and even passwords if they're transmitted in plaintext.

🔒 How to Defend:

✔ Always enable encryption (AES-128 or better) for wireless IIoT devices.

✔ Use frequency hopping to make signal interception harder.

✔ Implement whitelisting, so only trusted devices can communicate.

2️⃣ Active Attacks: Replay, Injection, and Jamming

Now things get serious. Attackers don't just listen—they manipulate.

☐ Replay Attacks (Faking Legitimate Commands)

Attackers record legitimate signals and rebroadcast them later. The system thinks the commands are coming from a trusted source, but they're actually being sent by an attacker.

✅ Example:

A hacker records the "open valve" command sent to an industrial control system.

Later, he replays it to force a valve open at the wrong time, causing a dangerous chemical spill.

💀 The Risk:

Even if your network uses authentication, replay attacks can bypass it because the system sees the replayed command as legitimate.

🔒 How to Defend:

✓ Use time-based tokens or nonces to prevent replay attacks.

✓ Implement device authentication to verify commands.

🎭 Packet Injection (Sending Fake Data to Industrial Devices)

Instead of replaying old data, an attacker crafts new malicious commands and injects them into the network.

✅ Example:

An attacker spoofs a factory temperature sensor to send fake "everything's fine" readings while the real temperature rises dangerously.

💀 The Risk:

Attackers can modify factory processes without triggering alarms.

They can sabotage production lines by feeding incorrect data into IIoT systems.

🔒 How to Defend:

✓ Use cryptographic message integrity checks to detect tampering.

✓ Segment wireless networks to prevent unauthorized access.

📡 Jamming Attacks (Denial-of-Service for IIoT Networks)

If an attacker can't hack you, they'll try to shut you down instead.

✅ Example:

A hacker floods the Zigbee frequency band with noise, causing all IIoT devices to lose connection.

Your smart factory goes dark, grinding production to a halt.

☠ The Risk:

Wireless jamming can take down entire production lines.

Attackers don't need to break in—they can jam your network from miles away.

🔒 How to Defend:

✔ Use frequency hopping to avoid sustained jamming.

✔ Implement wired backups for critical systems.

Tools of the Trade: How Attackers Sniff Wireless IIoT Traffic

Tool	What It Does	Why It's Dangerous
RTL-SDR	Cheap USB software-defined radio	Can intercept Zigbee, LoRa, and other IIoT signals
HackRF One	More advanced SDR with transmission capabilities	Can replay or inject malicious signals
GNU Radio	Software for decoding and analyzing wireless signals	Used for reverse-engineering industrial communication
Gqrx	SDR scanner for real-time signal monitoring	Helps attackers find active IIoT frequencies

Final Thoughts: Defending Your Wireless IIoT Systems

If your IIoT devices talk over the air, attackers can hear them—and mess with them. SDR gives hackers a cheap, powerful, and stealthy way to intercept and manipulate industrial networks. But here's the good news:

🔒 You can fight back!

✓ Encrypt EVERYTHING. Don't let attackers sniff plain-text communications.

✓ Use authentication. Ensure devices are who they say they are.

✓ Detect anomalies. Monitor network traffic for unusual behavior.

✓ Test your defenses. Use SDR tools to simulate attacks and find weak spots.

Because if you don't test your security, attackers will do it for you. 🚀

6.3 Jamming and Replay Attacks on Industrial Wireless Networks

The Silent Factory Takeover: When Your Machines Ignore You

Imagine walking into your state-of-the-art smart factory, only to find your robots frozen mid-task, conveyor belts halted, and every machine in eerie silence. Did the power go out? Nope. A hacker with a $30 radio device just jammed your wireless network.

Or worse—maybe the machines aren't frozen. Instead, they're following ghost commands, opening and closing valves, adjusting temperatures, or misreporting sensor data. No, this isn't a haunted factory. You've been hit by a replay attack—where an attacker captures legitimate signals and plays them back later to disrupt or hijack operations.

Both of these attacks are frighteningly easy to pull off and devastating to industrial environments. Whether it's a denial-of-service (DoS) via jamming or a covert manipulation via replay, industrial wireless networks are under constant threat—and it's time to fight back.

Understanding Jamming Attacks: When Your Factory Goes Radio Silent

What is Jamming?

Jamming is a brute-force attack that floods a wireless frequency with garbage signals, effectively drowning out legitimate communication. If your factory relies on Zigbee, LoRa, Wi-Fi, or 5G for IIoT operations, an attacker with the right tools can make sure your devices stop talking.

💀 Why Jamming is So Dangerous in IIoT

Total Factory Shutdown – Sensors, controllers, and industrial robots lose connection, halting operations.

Invisible Attack – There's no breach, no malware—just radio noise blocking communications.

Remote & Cheap – Attackers don't need access to your factory. They can jam you from outside your facility using a $100 SDR (software-defined radio).

How Hackers Jam Industrial Wireless Networks

◆ **Broadband Noise Jamming** – The attacker transmits random noise across the entire wireless spectrum used by IIoT devices.

◆ **Sweep Jamming** – A signal rapidly moves across frequencies, disrupting multiple channels one after another.

◆ **Reactive Jamming** – The attacker's SDR listens for legitimate signals and immediately transmits interference whenever it detects a transmission.

✅ Real-World Example:

A disgruntled ex-employee uses an SDR to jam Zigbee-based sensors in a warehouse, shutting down automated inventory tracking. The company spends days troubleshooting, thinking it's a hardware failure—until security cameras catch the guy parked outside with a laptop and a weird-looking antenna.

Defending Against Jamming Attacks

🔒 **Use Frequency Hopping (FHSS)** – Rapidly change frequencies so jammers can't keep up.

🔒 **Increase Signal Power** – Stronger signals are harder to jam (but watch out for interference).

🔒 **Deploy Wired Failovers** – Ensure critical devices have a wired backup if wireless fails.

🔒 **Install Jamming Detection Systems** – Use RF monitoring tools to detect unusual interference.

Replay Attacks: When Hackers Trick Your Machines into Obeying Old Commands

What is a Replay Attack?

A replay attack occurs when an attacker records legitimate IIoT communications (like a "start motor" command) and plays it back later to manipulate industrial processes.

✅ **Example Attack Scenario:**

1️⃣ A hacker sniffs an unencrypted Zigbee command that tells a robotic arm to move a product.

2️⃣ Later, the hacker replays the exact same signal, but at the wrong time—causing misalignment and assembly line chaos.

💀 **Why Replay Attacks are Dangerous**

They bypass authentication – If your system only checks if a signal is "valid" but not when it was sent, replay attacks work flawlessly.

They cause subtle, long-term damage – Unlike jamming, which is loud and obvious, replay attacks can go unnoticed for months.

Attackers don't need live access – Hackers can record data today and attack weeks later, making it hard to trace the source.

Defending Against Replay Attacks

🔒 **Use Time-Based Nonces** – Each command should have a timestamp or a one-time-use token. If the system sees an old timestamp, it rejects the command.

🔒 **Enable Message Authentication Codes (MACs)** – Ensure each wireless packet is signed and verified, preventing attackers from reusing old messages.

🔒 **Deploy End-to-End Encryption** – Encrypting IIoT traffic means attackers can't understand (or modify) intercepted commands.

Tools Attackers Use for Jamming & Replay Attacks

Tool	Used For	Why It's Dangerous
HackRF One	Jamming and replay attacks	Can jam Zigbee, LoRa, and Wi-Fi
BladeRF	Advanced SDR attacks	Can spoof IIoT signals
RTL-SDR	Passive signal sniffing	Cheap and widely available
Flipper Zero	Capturing and replaying signals	Small, portable, and easy to use

Wireless IIoT networks are incredibly powerful—but also incredibly vulnerable. Attackers don't need to break into your factory physically. They can disrupt operations from a parking lot with just a radio and a laptop.

🚀 **Take Action Today:**

✓ Encrypt your wireless traffic to prevent replay attacks.

✓ Use frequency hopping to evade jammers.

✓ Deploy jamming detection systems before attackers exploit you.

✓ Test your own security with SDR tools—before hackers do.

Because in cybersecurity, the only thing scarier than a ghost in the machine is a hacker in the parking lot. 🚗📡

6.4 Exploiting Weak Authentication in RFID and NFC Systems

The Accidental Hacker: How a $5 Device Can Ruin Your Security

Imagine this: You walk into a high-security industrial facility, flash your badge, and the RFID reader beeps in approval. The door clicks open. All good, right?

Now picture this: A hacker, casually standing behind you with a $5 RFID cloner in his pocket, just copied your badge wirelessly. Next time, he won't need to tailgate—he'll walk right in, badge in hand, looking just like an authorized employee.

Welcome to the terrifyingly easy world of RFID and NFC hacking. Whether it's cloning employee badges, manipulating industrial NFC-based controls, or skimming contactless payment cards, weak authentication in RFID and NFC systems is a goldmine for attackers. And the worst part? Most systems don't even realize they've been compromised.

Let's break down how attackers exploit weak authentication, how they clone, replay, and manipulate data, and, most importantly—how to stop them before they waltz into your factory with a fake badge.

Understanding RFID and NFC in Industrial Security

What Are RFID and NFC?

RFID (Radio Frequency Identification): Uses radio waves to identify and track assets, employees, or industrial equipment. Common in employee badges, asset tracking, and inventory control.

NFC (Near Field Communication): A type of RFID that requires close proximity (a few centimeters). Used in contactless payments, industrial control panels, and secure access.

Why are these technologies a security nightmare?

Many RFID systems still use weak encryption or no encryption at all.

Authentication is often just an ID number—easily cloned and replayed.

Legacy industrial access systems don't check for anomalies, making them blind to unauthorized use.

How Hackers Exploit Weak RFID and NFC Authentication

1. Cloning RFID Badges & Access Cards

◆ The Attack:

Using a handheld RFID reader (like the infamous Proxmark3), a hacker can scan and copy an employee's badge in seconds. Once cloned, they can create a duplicate badge and walk in like they belong.

◆ Real-World Example:

A security researcher used a long-range RFID reader hidden in a backpack to steal dozens of employee badges just by walking past them. Employees never even knew their badges were copied.

☐ Defensive Strategies:

✓ **Use Secure RFID Standards** – Upgrade from 125kHz (low-frequency, easily cloned) to encrypted 13.56MHz (MIFARE DESFire, iCLASS SE).
✓ **Enable Multi-Factor Authentication (MFA)** – Combine RFID with a PIN, biometric scan, or one-time passcode.
✓ **Monitor for Duplicate Badge Activity** – If two identical IDs show up in different places, you've got a problem.

2. Relay Attacks on NFC-Based Access Systems

◆ The Attack:

An attacker relays an NFC signal from an authorized user to a remote attacker who then gains access. This effectively tricks the system into thinking the attacker is standing at the access point.

◆ Example:

A hacker sits outside an industrial facility and secretly relays an employee's NFC signal to an accomplice inside the building, who then gains entry.

☐ Defensive Strategies:

✅ **Use Time-Based Challenges** – Limit authentication to a short window, blocking relayed signals.

✅ **Detect Unusual Signal Strengths** – If an NFC badge is being read from an unnatural distance, block access.

✅ **Use Bluetooth or Ultra-Wideband (UWB) for Authentication** – Harder to relay than NFC.

3. Skimming & Data Manipulation Attacks on Industrial NFC Systems

◆ **The Attack:**

Some industrial control panels use NFC for machine authentication—but if the system doesn't verify the integrity of the NFC data, an attacker can modify or inject commands.

◆ **Example:**

A hacker modifies an NFC tag on a smart factory machine, tricking it into running unauthorized processes or disabling security controls.

☐ **Defensive Strategies:**

✅ **Sign and Encrypt NFC Data** – Prevents tampering or injection.

✅ **Authenticate NFC Tags with a Secure Backend** – Don't trust static, hardcoded tag data.

✅ **Use NFC Kill Switches** – Physically disable compromised NFC readers.

Tools Attackers Use to Exploit RFID and NFC

Tool	What It Does	Why It's Dangerous
Proxmark3	Reads, clones, and emulates RFID cards	Can copy badges in seconds
ChameleonMini	Stores and emulates multiple RFID tags	Allows for on-the-fly card switching
Flipper Zero	Scans, clones, and replays RFID and NFC	Small, portable, easy to use
HackRF One	Intercepts and manipulates NFC signals	Can relay NFC credentials from a distance

The Future of RFID & NFC Security in Industrial Systems

RFID and NFC are incredibly useful for industrial security and automation—but only when implemented correctly. The problem? Most factories and enterprises are still using outdated, weak authentication methods that attackers can bypass with minimal effort.

🚀 **What You Should Do Today:**

✅ Encrypt and sign all RFID and NFC communications.

✅ Use multifactor authentication instead of relying only on badges.

✅ Upgrade from weak 125kHz systems to secure 13.56MHz solutions.

✅ Regularly scan for unauthorized or duplicate RFID credentials.

Because let's face it—if a $5 device from Amazon can break into your factory, you have bigger problems than just lost productivity. 🔥

6.5 Protecting IIoT Wireless Communications Against Cyber Threats

The Wi-Fi Nightmare: When Your Factory Talks Too Much

Picture this: A hacker parks a van outside your state-of-the-art smart factory, opens a laptop, and with a few clicks, hijacks your entire wireless network. Machines malfunction, robotic arms start moving like they're possessed, and your SCADA system starts speaking in binary gibberish.

No, this isn't some Hollywood cyber-thriller—it's what happens when industrial IoT (IIoT) wireless networks are left vulnerable to cyber threats. With everything from automated assembly lines to sensor-driven logistics relying on wireless communication, a single security flaw can bring down an entire operation.

So how do we keep IIoT wireless networks locked down tighter than Fort Knox? Let's break it down.

The Wireless Battlefield in Industrial IoT

Industrial IoT environments use a variety of wireless protocols, each with unique vulnerabilities. Here's what we're dealing with:

1. Wi-Fi (802.11x)

Used for general connectivity, remote monitoring, and data transfer.

Vulnerabilities: Weak encryption, rogue AP attacks, packet sniffing, deauthentication attacks.

2. Zigbee & Z-Wave

Common in sensor networks, industrial automation, and smart energy management.

Vulnerabilities: Unencrypted traffic, weak key management, easily jammed signals.

3. LoRaWAN & LPWAN

Used for long-range, low-power communications (e.g., remote monitoring of pipelines, agriculture).

Vulnerabilities: Lack of authentication, easy replay attacks, signal hijacking.

4. 5G & Private LTE

Increasingly used in smart factories for high-speed, low-latency connectivity.

Vulnerabilities: SIM cloning, IMSI catchers (fake base stations), protocol exploitation.

Every wireless protocol in IIoT expands the attack surface, making it a prime target for hackers. Let's dive into the most common wireless attacks and how to stop them.

Common Cyber Threats Targeting IIoT Wireless Communications

1. Rogue Access Points (Evil Twin Attacks)

◆ **The Attack:**

A hacker sets up a fake Wi-Fi network with the same SSID as your factory's legitimate network. Employees and devices unknowingly connect, exposing sensitive industrial data.

◆ How to Prevent It:

✓ Use WPA3 encryption and disable WEP/WPA1 (seriously, it's 2025—stop using outdated protocols).

✓ Enable network authentication with certificates.

✓ Use Wireless Intrusion Detection Systems (WIDS) to detect rogue APs.

2. Deauthentication Attacks (Wi-Fi Jamming)

◆ The Attack:

Hackers send deauth packets to disconnect IIoT devices from the network, causing disruptions.

◆ How to Prevent It:

✓ Use WPA3 and Management Frame Protection (MFP) to block spoofed deauth packets.

✓ Use frequency hopping or redundant backup connections for critical devices.

3. Sniffing and MITM Attacks

◆ The Attack:

Hackers intercept unencrypted traffic, capturing credentials, sensor data, and control signals.

◆ How to Prevent It:

✓ Always encrypt wireless traffic (AES-256 for Zigbee, VPN tunnels for Wi-Fi).

✓ Use TLS 1.3 for MQTT and OPC-UA communications.

✅ Monitor network traffic for anomalies.

4. Jamming and Denial-of-Service (DoS)

◆ The Attack:

Hackers flood IIoT wireless networks with noise, disrupting sensor communication and automation processes.

◆ How to Prevent It:

✅ Use frequency-hopping spread spectrum (FHSS) and direct-sequence spread spectrum (DSSS) to resist jamming.

✅ Deploy redundant wired connections for critical infrastructure.

✅ Use spectrum monitoring tools to detect unusual RF interference.

5. Replay Attacks on LoRaWAN & Zigbee

◆ The Attack:

Hackers capture and replay legitimate commands to control industrial devices.

◆ How to Prevent It:

✅ Use cryptographic nonces and rolling codes to prevent replay attacks.

✅ Disable default keys and implement strong authentication.

Best Practices for Securing IIoT Wireless Communications

1. Encrypt Everything

Use AES-256 encryption for Wi-Fi, Zigbee, and LoRaWAN.

Enable TLS 1.3 or VPN tunnels for all wireless data transmissions.

2. Implement Strong Authentication

Use certificate-based authentication for Wi-Fi (EAP-TLS).

Enforce multi-factor authentication (MFA) for device access.

Rotate network encryption keys frequently.

3. Monitor and Detect Wireless Threats

Deploy Wireless Intrusion Detection/Prevention Systems (WIDS/WIPS).

Regularly scan for rogue access points and unauthorized devices.

Analyze network traffic for suspicious behavior.

4. Segment Wireless IIoT Networks

Separate OT networks from IT networks using VLANs and firewalls.

Isolate critical devices on dedicated frequency bands.

5. Conduct Regular Security Audits

Perform penetration testing on IIoT wireless networks.

Assess default settings and disable insecure protocols.

Train employees to recognize and report suspicious activity.

Final Thoughts: Wireless Security Is Not Optional

Let's be real—if your IIoT wireless network can be hacked by a teenager with a Raspberry Pi, you're asking for trouble. Attackers love unprotected wireless devices, and industrial environments are filled with golden opportunities for cyber threats.

✓ Encrypt, authenticate, monitor, and segment your networks.

✓ Harden your wireless protocols before hackers do it for you.

✓ Test your security regularly—because the bad guys definitely are.

Because at the end of the day, a well-secured IIoT wireless network means fewer cyber nightmares and more industrial uptime. And let's be honest—that's what we all want. 🚀

Chapter 7: Exploiting ICS/SCADA Communication Protocols

ICS communication protocols were designed for reliability, not security. That's why attackers love them. Modbus, DNP3, OPC-UA—these protocols trust everything and verify nothing, making them prime targets for MITM attacks, replay attacks, and protocol hijacking. In the wrong hands, a simple packet manipulation can cause a power grid failure, disrupt an oil refinery, or bring an entire factory to a standstill.

This chapter explores common ICS communication protocols, their inherent security weaknesses, and how attackers exploit them. We'll discuss case studies like Stuxnet, the dangers of replay and injection attacks, and the steps organizations can take to secure industrial protocol communications against tampering and exploitation.

7.1 MITM Attacks on Modbus, DNP3, and PROFINET Communications

Welcome to the Middle of the Cyber Warzone!

Imagine you're running a high-tech smart factory, pumping out thousands of precision-engineered widgets a day. Everything is automated, the machines talk to each other using industrial communication protocols, and life is good. Until it isn't.

One day, a rogue engineer (or a cybercriminal parked outside your facility) silently hijacks your industrial control system (ICS) communications. Your perfectly fine factory starts acting weird—temperature sensors send bogus readings, pumps switch off randomly, and the robotic arms? They're either on strike or moving like they've been possessed by a poltergeist.

Congratulations! You've just become the latest victim of a Man-in-the-Middle (MITM) attack on industrial protocols like Modbus, DNP3, and PROFINET. And trust me, if you're not securing these critical communication channels, it's only a matter of time before it happens to you.

So, what exactly is a MITM attack in industrial networks, and how do we stop it? Let's dive in.

What is a MITM Attack in ICS?

A Man-in-the-Middle (MITM) attack is when an attacker secretly intercepts, manipulates, or injects malicious commands between two communicating devices—without either of them knowing. In industrial environments, this means an attacker could:

◆ Alter sensor readings (e.g., make a temperature sensor report normal values while the machine is overheating).

◆ Inject malicious control commands (e.g., shut down a water pump or over-speed a motor).

◆ Silently eavesdrop on process data to gather intelligence for a future cyberattack.

Now, let's break down how these attacks work on Modbus, DNP3, and PROFINET, the protocols that keep factories, power grids, and critical infrastructure running.

How MITM Attacks Work in Modbus, DNP3, and PROFINET

1. Modbus: The Security Nightmare That Just Won't Die

Modbus is one of the oldest and most widely used industrial communication protocols. Unfortunately, it was designed in the 1970s, when cybersecurity wasn't even a concept.

🔥 Why Modbus is Vulnerable to MITM Attacks:

✗ No encryption—all data is sent in plaintext.

✗ No authentication—any device can send commands if it has network access.

✗ No integrity checks—attackers can modify packets without detection.

☐☠☐ How Attackers Exploit Modbus in MITM Attacks:

Packet Sniffing: Hackers intercept Modbus traffic and read data like temperature, pressure, and system status.

Command Injection: Attackers send malicious commands, such as turning off a motor or changing sensor readings.

Response Manipulation: The hacker modifies responses from devices to make operators believe everything is normal—while the system is actually failing.

✅ How to Defend Against MITM in Modbus:

🔒 Use VPNs or TLS-encrypted Modbus gateways to encrypt traffic.

🔒 Implement firewall rules to block unauthorized devices from sending Modbus commands.

🔒 Use intrusion detection systems (IDS) to flag abnormal Modbus traffic.

2. DNP3: Built for Reliability, Not Security

DNP3 (Distributed Network Protocol 3) is popular in the electric grid, water utilities, and SCADA systems. It was designed for reliability, but unfortunately, not for security.

🔥 Why DNP3 is Vulnerable to MITM Attacks:

✖ Original versions lack encryption (DNP3 over TCP/IP sends plaintext messages).

✖ Delayed authentication—if authentication is used, it often happens after the connection is established.

✖ Critical commands can be altered mid-transmission.

☠ How Attackers Exploit DNP3 in MITM Attacks:

Data Interception: Hackers eavesdrop on SCADA-to-RTU (Remote Terminal Unit) communications to steal data.

Response Tampering: Attackers modify circuit breaker status messages, tricking operators into thinking a system is on or off.

Command Injection: Hackers remotely trigger shutdowns or overloads in a power grid.

✅ How to Defend Against MITM in DNP3:

🔒 Use DNP3 Secure Authentication (DNP3-SA) to enforce message integrity.

🔒 Encrypt DNP3 communications with VPNs or IPSec.

🔒 Implement anomaly detection systems to catch unexpected DNP3 traffic.

3. PROFINET: Fast, Flexible, and Targeted by Hackers

PROFINET is a widely used Ethernet-based protocol in industrial automation. While it's fast and efficient, its security depends entirely on proper configuration.

🔥 Why PROFINET is Vulnerable to MITM Attacks:

✗ Uses standard Ethernet, making it vulnerable to common network attacks.

✗ Devices can be impersonated, allowing attackers to inject malicious commands.

✗ Man-in-the-Middle attacks can disrupt industrial automation workflows.

☠ How Attackers Exploit PROFINET in MITM Attacks:

Packet Sniffing: Attackers intercept and read real-time control commands.

Device Spoofing: A hacker pretends to be a PLC (Programmable Logic Controller) and issues unauthorized commands.

Data Manipulation: Attackers modify sensor readings to cause operational failures.

✅ How to Defend Against MITM in PROFINET:

🔒 Use PROFINET Security Class 3, which enforces authentication and encryption.
🔒 Segment PROFINET traffic using VLANs to isolate critical devices.
🔒 Deploy Intrusion Prevention Systems (IPS) to detect MITM attempts.

Stopping MITM Attacks in Industrial Networks

MITM attacks thrive in weakly secured industrial networks. Here's how you shut them down:

1. Encrypt All Communications

🔒 Use VPNs, TLS, or IPSec tunnels for Modbus, DNP3, and PROFINET.

2. Use Strong Authentication

🔒 Implement DNP3-SA, certificate-based authentication, and device whitelisting.

3. Segment Industrial Networks

🔒 Keep SCADA, OT, and IT networks separate using VLANs and firewalls.

4. Monitor for Suspicious Traffic

🔒 Use IDS/IPS systems to detect unexpected protocol behavior.

5. Conduct Regular Penetration Testing

🔒 Simulate MITM attacks to test your defenses and patch vulnerabilities.

Final Thoughts: The MITM Apocalypse is Avoidable

Hackers love insecure industrial protocols. Modbus, DNP3, and PROFINET were never built with security in mind, but that doesn't mean we have to roll out the red carpet for attackers.

If your industrial network is unprotected, you're basically inviting cybercriminals to a free buffet of exploits. But with the right encryption, authentication, and monitoring, you can kick MITM attackers out of your system—before they turn your factory into a hacker's playground.

So, do yourself (and your machines) a favor: secure your industrial protocols, or prepare for chaos. 🚀

7.2 Replay and Injection Attacks on ICS Protocols

The Cybersecurity Time Machine: How Attackers Trick Your Industrial Systems

Imagine if you could rewind time and replay the best moments of your life whenever you wanted. First job promotion? Play it again! That time you accidentally ate two pizzas in one sitting? Yep, let's relive it.

Well, hackers love replaying things too—except instead of reliving nostalgic memories, they're replaying industrial control system (ICS) commands to sabotage operations.

Welcome to replay and injection attacks, where cybercriminals record valid commands and later replay or inject their own malicious versions to disrupt industrial processes.

Think of it like someone recording your voice saying, "Turn off the lights," and then playing it back later to shut down your entire factory, power grid, or water treatment plant. Scary? Absolutely. Avoidable? 100%. Let's break down how these attacks work and how to stop them.

What Are Replay and Injection Attacks?

A Replay Attack is when an attacker captures a legitimate data packet (such as a sensor reading or a control command) and replays it later to cause unintended behavior.

An Injection Attack is when an attacker modifies or creates new malicious packets and injects them into the system to manipulate industrial processes.

These attacks are particularly dangerous in ICS environments where real-time control is critical. Imagine a hacker replaying a valve open command over and over, flooding a chemical plant. Or injecting a shutdown signal into a power grid.

How Replay and Injection Attacks Work in ICS Protocols

1. Modbus: The Sitting Duck of ICS Security

Modbus is a common industrial protocol that's as secure as a diary with no lock. It lacks encryption, authentication, and integrity checks, making it a hacker's dream target.

☐☠☐ How Attackers Exploit Modbus with Replay & Injection:

Step 1: Capture a valid Modbus command, such as "Turn off motor 3".

Step 2: Replay the command later, shutting down the motor at will.

Step 3: Modify a packet to say "Increase boiler temperature to 500°C" (even though it should never exceed 100°C).

✅ How to Defend Against Replay & Injection on Modbus:

🔒 Upgrade to Modbus Secure (TLS encryption).
🔒 Use network segmentation to isolate Modbus devices from unauthorized access.

🔒 Implement firewalls and intrusion detection to detect abnormal Modbus traffic.

2. DNP3: Secure-ish, But Still Vulnerable

DNP3 is more secure than Modbus, but older implementations still lack encryption and authentication. Attackers can manipulate SCADA communications, replaying shutdown commands or injecting false sensor data.

☠ How Attackers Exploit DNP3:

Step 1: Capture a real DNP3 response packet, such as "Breaker Status: Open".

Step 2: Replay it to make operators believe a breaker is open—even if it's actually closed.

Step 3: Inject fake sensor readings to trick SCADA into making bad decisions.

✅ How to Defend Against Replay & Injection on DNP3:

🔒 Enable DNP3 Secure Authentication (DNP3-SA) to prevent replay attacks.
🔒 Encrypt DNP3 traffic using VPNs or IPSec.
🔒 Use anomaly detection tools to spot unusual DNP3 traffic patterns.

3. PROFINET: The High-Speed Target

PROFINET is an Ethernet-based protocol used in industrial automation. Since it's built on standard networking, it's vulnerable to packet sniffing, replay, and injection attacks.

☠ How Attackers Exploit PROFINET:

Step 1: Record a valid control command like "Move robotic arm to position A".

Step 2: Replay the command at the wrong time, causing a robotic malfunction.

Step 3: Inject a command to disable safety mechanisms, leading to potential damage.

✅ How to Defend Against Replay & Injection on PROFINET:

🔒 Use PROFINET Security Class 3, which includes authentication and encryption.

🔒 Implement Access Control Lists (ACLs) to restrict PROFINET traffic.

🔒 Deploy intrusion prevention systems (IPS) to detect and block malicious PROFINET commands.

Real-World ICS Attacks Using Replay & Injection

Stuxnet: The King of Injection Attacks

Stuxnet, the famous cyberweapon that sabotaged Iran's nuclear program, used command injection to make centrifuges spin at destructive speeds—while feeding operators false sensor data to hide the attack.

The Ukrainian Power Grid Attack (2015 & 2016)

Hackers used replay and injection attacks to remotely disable circuit breakers, cutting power for hundreds of thousands of people.

Triton (Trisis) Attack on Saudi Petrochemical Plant (2017)

A hacker group attempted to inject malicious commands into safety instrumented systems (SIS) to cause catastrophic failure.

How to Defend Against Replay & Injection Attacks in ICS

1. Implement Secure Protocols

🔒 Use DNP3-SA, Modbus Secure, and PROFINET Security Class 3 to add encryption and authentication.

2. Enable Cryptographic Integrity Checks

🔒 Deploy message authentication codes (MACs) to ensure messages haven't been altered.

3. Use Time-Based Anti-Replay Mechanisms

🔒 Implement timestamp validation to reject old or replayed commands.

4. Monitor for Abnormal Command Patterns

🔒 Use intrusion detection systems (IDS) to flag repeated or unexpected commands.

5. Apply Network Segmentation and Zero Trust

🔒 Keep SCADA, OT, and IT networks separate with firewalls and access controls.

6. Conduct Regular Security Audits

🔒 Test for replay and injection vulnerabilities in your ICS systems with red team exercises.

Final Thoughts: Hackers Love a Good Replay—So Don't Let Them

Replay and injection attacks in ICS networks are like cyber time machines for hackers—letting them control industrial processes at will. Whether it's Modbus, DNP3, or PROFINET, if your system lacks encryption and authentication, you're an easy target.

But good news! Defending against these attacks isn't rocket science (unless you're protecting a rocket factory). Encrypt, authenticate, segment, and monitor your network—and those sneaky hackers won't stand a chance. 🚀

7.3 Attacking and Hijacking OPC-UA and MQTT Broker Communications

Breaking into the Nerve Centers of IIoT

Picture this: You're sitting in a control room, sipping your coffee, when suddenly—BOOM! The entire factory grinds to a halt. Machines stop mid-cycle, alarms go haywire, and the boss is storming in demanding answers. Turns out, a hacker hijacked your OPC-UA and MQTT communications, injecting false data and seizing control of critical industrial processes.

Welcome to the wild west of industrial IoT (IIoT) protocols—where attackers don't just break in, they rewrite reality. Today, we're diving deep into how hackers exploit OPC-UA and MQTT, and more importantly, how you can stop them before they turn your factory into a scene from a cyber-thriller.

Understanding OPC-UA and MQTT: The Backbone of IIoT Communication

OPC-UA (Open Platform Communications Unified Architecture) and MQTT (Message Queuing Telemetry Transport) are two of the most widely used protocols for industrial automation and IIoT.

OPC-UA is the go-to industrial protocol for secure, real-time data exchange between machines, SCADA systems, and cloud platforms. It's structured, scalable, and designed with built-in security features (but let's be honest—many companies don't use them properly).

MQTT is a lightweight publish-subscribe messaging protocol, widely used in IIoT environments, from smart factories to power grids. It's efficient, flexible, and easy to deploy, but it's also a hacker's paradise when misconfigured.

Both protocols keep modern industrial systems running—which makes them prime targets for cyberattacks. Let's break down how hackers infiltrate and hijack them.

How Hackers Exploit OPC-UA Communications

1. Man-in-the-Middle (MITM) Attacks on OPC-UA

Even though OPC-UA supports encryption and authentication, many organizations disable security features for "performance reasons." This is like installing a front door but removing the lock because it slows you down.

☐☠☐ **How Attackers Exploit OPC-UA with MITM:**

Step 1: The attacker intercepts unencrypted OPC-UA traffic.

Step 2: They modify data in transit (e.g., fake sensor readings or control commands).

Step 3: The manipulated data reaches SCADA/HMI systems, causing operators to make wrong decisions or automated systems to fail catastrophically.

✓ How to Defend Against MITM on OPC-UA:

🔒 Enable TLS encryption—no excuses.
🔒 Use digital certificates to authenticate trusted devices.
🔒 Monitor OPC-UA traffic for anomalies and unauthorized access.

2. OPC-UA Credential Theft and Session Hijacking

Attackers can steal weak or default credentials, then hijack an active OPC-UA session to issue malicious commands. This is game over for your industrial process.

☐☠☐ How Attackers Hijack OPC-UA Sessions:

Step 1: Brute-force or steal OPC-UA user credentials.

Step 2: Authenticate into the OPC-UA server and impersonate a legitimate user.

Step 3: Send malicious commands (e.g., shut down production lines or disable safety systems).

✅ How to Prevent OPC-UA Credential Theft & Hijacking:

🔒 Enforce strong authentication policies (passwords + certificates).
🔒 Implement role-based access control (RBAC) to limit access.
🔒 Enable session timeout and re-authentication to prevent long-term hijacking.

How Hackers Exploit MQTT Broker Communications

1. Unsecured MQTT Brokers: The Open Door to Mayhem

Many MQTT brokers are left wide open on the internet, with no authentication, no encryption, and no access controls. Attackers can subscribe to topics, publish fake data, or even shut down entire IIoT systems.

☐☠☐ How Attackers Exploit Open MQTT Brokers:

Step 1: Scan for open MQTT brokers using Shodan or Censys.

Step 2: Connect as a malicious subscriber and eavesdrop on industrial data.

Step 3: Publish false commands (e.g., "Emergency shutdown: ALL SYSTEMS OFF").

✅ How to Secure MQTT Brokers:

🔒 Require authentication and authorization for all connections.
🔒 Use TLS encryption to secure message transport.
🔒 Disable anonymous access and set up strict ACLs (Access Control Lists).

2. Payload Injection Attacks: Feeding MQTT Bad Data

MQTT messages often contain critical operational data (temperature, pressure, machine status, etc.). If an attacker injects fake values, it can lead to dangerous consequences.

☠️ How Payload Injection Attacks Work:

Step 1: Attacker hijacks an MQTT client or exploits weak authentication.

Step 2: Injects malicious payloads into messages (e.g., "Temperature = 2000°C").

Step 3: The system responds to the fake data, causing operational failure or safety hazards.

✅ How to Prevent MQTT Payload Injection:

🔒 Implement message integrity checks (signatures, hashing).
🔒 Use publish-subscribe filtering to block unexpected data changes.
🔒 Set up anomaly detection alerts for abnormal data values.

Real-World OPC-UA & MQTT Attacks

2019 Water Treatment Facility Hack

Attackers exploited weak OPC-UA security to remotely control water chemical levels, nearly poisoning an entire town.

2021 MQTT Smart Factory Breach

A misconfigured MQTT broker exposed factory sensor data to the internet, allowing attackers to inject false commands and disrupt production.

2022 Oil Refinery Cyberattack

Hackers used MQTT injection to disable safety systems, forcing a manual emergency shutdown of the refinery.

How to Defend OPC-UA and MQTT from Cyberattacks

1. Always Encrypt Traffic

🔒 Use TLS encryption for OPC-UA and MQTT communications.

2. Implement Strong Authentication

🔒 Require certificates, usernames/passwords, or multi-factor authentication (MFA).

3. Segment Your Networks

🔒 Keep MQTT brokers and OPC-UA servers isolated from public networks.

4. Monitor for Anomalies

🔒 Use SIEM (Security Information and Event Management) tools to detect unusual activity.

5. Disable Anonymous Access

🔒 Block unauthenticated connections to MQTT brokers and OPC-UA servers.

Final Thoughts: Don't Let Hackers Hijack Your IIoT Brain

If your IIoT environment runs on OPC-UA or MQTT, securing them is non-negotiable. These protocols are the brains of industrial automation, and if hackers gain control, they can manipulate your entire operation.

So lock it down—encrypt, authenticate, segment, and monitor. Because if a hacker gets in, your machines won't be working for you anymore... they'll be working for them. 🔐

7.4 Case Study: Stuxnet and Protocol Manipulation in ICS

The Stuxnet Saga: When Cyberwarfare Went Industrial

Alright, grab some popcorn, because this isn't just another malware story—it's the Hollywood blockbuster of industrial cyberattacks. Picture this: A highly sophisticated, government-backed piece of malware sneaks its way into a top-secret nuclear facility, silently manipulates industrial control protocols, and causes physical destruction—all without triggering any alarms. Sounds like a cyber-thriller, right?

Well, welcome to Stuxnet, the world's first true cyberweapon. It wasn't just designed to steal data or disrupt networks—it was crafted to physically sabotage industrial equipment by exploiting SCADA and PLC communication protocols. And here's the scary part: The tactics Stuxnet used are still being studied, replicated, and evolved today.

So, let's break down how Stuxnet worked, why it was so deadly, and what it means for Industrial IoT (IIoT) and SCADA security today.

Stuxnet: The Malware That Changed Cybersecurity Forever

Stuxnet wasn't some script kiddie's pet project—it was one of the most sophisticated cyber weapons ever created. Discovered in 2010, it was designed to infiltrate Iran's Natanz nuclear enrichment facility and sabotage centrifuges used for uranium enrichment.

What made Stuxnet legendary?

It Spread Like a Worm, But Attacked Like a Sniper

Unlike typical malware that spreads chaotically, Stuxnet was highly targeted.

It infected hundreds of thousands of computers but only activated on specific Siemens PLCs controlling centrifuges.

It Manipulated Industrial Protocols to Cause Physical Damage

Stuxnet intercepted and manipulated PLC commands.

It made centrifuges spin at unstable speeds, causing them to break down while showing normal readings to operators.

It Exploited Zero-Day Vulnerabilities

Stuxnet leveraged four zero-day exploits—a level of sophistication rare even in state-sponsored attacks.

It bypassed Microsoft Windows security, Siemens Step7 software, and USB air-gapped defenses.

It Used Rootkits to Stay Hidden

Stuxnet was designed to be stealthy. It altered data so that operators saw everything running smoothly, even as equipment was being physically destroyed.

The result? Over 1,000 centrifuges were physically damaged, slowing down Iran's nuclear program by years.

How Did Stuxnet Manipulate ICS/SCADA Protocols?

Now, here's where it gets terrifying: Stuxnet wasn't just a virus—it was a master of protocol manipulation.

1. Man-in-the-Middle (MITM) Attack on PLC Communication

Stuxnet injected itself between the Siemens Step7 software and the PLCs, acting as a MITM attacker.

What it did: Intercepted normal PLC commands, altered them, and sent fake data back to the operator.

Result: Operators saw "everything is fine" while centrifuges were self-destructing.

2. Exploiting Siemens PLC Firmware

Stuxnet rewrote PLC logic to introduce faulty speed control commands:

It slowed centrifuges down below operating levels (507 Hz).

Then spun them up dangerously fast (1410 Hz).

Finally, restored normal speeds—repeating the cycle until mechanical failure occurred.

3. Hiding Its Tracks with a Rootkit

Normally, when equipment malfunctions, operators see warning signs. Not with Stuxnet.

Stuxnet intercepted monitoring data and fed fake "all clear" signals to SCADA systems.

The entire sabotage happened in plain sight, with no alarms triggered.

This wasn't just hacking—this was cyber warfare precision-engineered for destruction.

The Aftermath: What Stuxnet Means for IIoT Security Today

The Stuxnet attack changed the game. It proved that cyberattacks can cause real-world physical destruction—and that ICS/SCADA systems are prime targets.

What Stuxnet Taught Us About Industrial Cybersecurity

Air-Gapping Isn't Enough

The Natanz facility was air-gapped (isolated from the internet).

Stuxnet still got in via USB flash drives.

Lesson: Don't assume isolation = security.

Industrial Protocols Were Never Designed for Security

SCADA and PLCs prioritize efficiency over security.

They lack authentication and encryption by default.

Lesson: Industrial networks need modern security measures—firewalls, anomaly detection, and real-time monitoring.

Attackers Can Manipulate Data to Hide Their Tracks

Stuxnet spoofed sensor data, making operators believe everything was fine.

Lesson: Trusting raw data from ICS protocols without integrity checks is dangerous.

State-Sponsored Cyber Warfare is Real

Stuxnet showed that nation-states are willing to use malware as a weapon.

Today, similar tactics are being used by hackers targeting power grids, oil refineries, and smart factories.

How to Defend Against Stuxnet-Style Attacks in Modern IIoT Systems

✓ **1. Secure SCADA & PLC Communications**

🔒 Implement network segmentation (keep IT & OT separate).
🔒 Use encrypted communication protocols for SCADA data.
🔒 Enable role-based access control (RBAC) on PLCs.

✓ **2. Monitor for Anomalous Behavior**

🔒 Deploy intrusion detection systems (IDS) for ICS networks.
🔒 Use AI-powered anomaly detection to spot unusual control commands.

✓ **3. Protect Against Firmware Manipulation**

🔒 Regularly update PLC firmware and apply patches.
🔒 Validate firmware integrity checks before deployment.

✓ **4. Control Physical & USB Access**

🔒 Disable USB ports on industrial systems.
🔒 Implement USB scanning stations to check for malware.

✓ **5. Implement Zero Trust Security**

🔒 Assume attackers are already inside and verify every device.
🔒 Require multi-factor authentication (MFA) for SCADA access.

Final Thoughts: The Legacy of Stuxnet

Stuxnet was just the beginning of industrial cyber warfare. Today, we see ransomware targeting pipelines, attacks on smart grids, and hackers breaching smart factories. The next Stuxnet won't just attack nuclear facilities—it will target energy grids, transportation systems, and water treatment plants.

The key lesson? Industrial systems were never built for security, but they must be secured.

So if you're running IIoT, SCADA, or smart factory systems—treat cybersecurity as a priority, not an afterthought. Because the next Stuxnet is already being written somewhere, and you don't want to be its next target. 🚨

7.5 Securing Industrial Communication Protocols from Cyber Attacks

Welcome to the Industrial Cyber Battleground

Picture this: You're running a smart factory, everything's humming along smoothly—robots assembling parts, conveyor belts rolling, sensors tracking efficiency. Then, out of nowhere, your entire system goes haywire. Machines overheat, sensors go blind, and your once-automated paradise turns into a digital dumpster fire. What happened?

Hackers happened.

They infiltrated your industrial communication protocols—Modbus, DNP3, OPC-UA, MQTT—injecting malicious commands, rerouting traffic, and even spoofing sensor data. Your perfectly tuned operation? Now it's a hacker's playground.

If that scenario sounds like a nightmare, that's because it is. And it's happening more often than you think. So let's get real about how to lock down your industrial communication protocols before hackers turn your smart factory into a smart disaster.

Why Industrial Protocols Are So Vulnerable

Here's the problem: Most industrial protocols were never designed with security in mind.

When SCADA systems were first developed, they were meant to work in isolated environments—closed networks, no internet, no outside threats. Cybersecurity wasn't even a consideration. Then IoT happened. Now, industrial networks are connected, remote access is the norm, and suddenly, protocols designed in the 1970s are exposed to 21st-century cyberattacks.

Common Security Weaknesses in Industrial Protocols

● **No Built-in Encryption**: Most ICS/SCADA protocols (Modbus, DNP3) send data in plain text. That means attackers can intercept and modify commands.

● **Lack of Authentication**: Many legacy systems don't verify who's sending commands. If a hacker gets in, they can impersonate legitimate devices and wreak havoc.

● **Weak Access Controls**: ICS systems often lack user authentication mechanisms. If someone gains access, they have free rein over critical systems.

● **Trust-Based Networks**: Many industrial networks assume that all devices are trustworthy—a dream scenario for attackers who love to inject malicious traffic undetected.

Top Cyber Threats to Industrial Protocols

Understanding how attackers exploit ICS protocols is the first step in securing them. Here are some of the nastiest attacks to watch out for:

1. Man-in-the-Middle (MITM) Attacks

Attackers intercept and alter communication between devices.

They can modify sensor data, making operators believe everything is fine while systems are being sabotaged.

Common targets: Modbus, DNP3, OPC-UA.

2. Command Injection Attacks

Hackers send unauthorized control commands to PLCs and SCADA systems.

Example: A hacker can inject a command to shut down a power grid or overheat a machine.

Common targets: Modbus, PROFINET, BACnet.

3. Replay Attacks

Attackers capture legitimate commands and replay them later to manipulate devices.

Example: A hacker records a valve's "open" command and replays it later to cause a flood.

Common targets: DNP3, IEC 61850, MQTT.

4. Rogue Device Injection

Attackers introduce unauthorized devices into the network to send malicious commands.

Common targets: All ICS protocols that lack device authentication.

5. Denial-of-Service (DoS) Attacks

Hackers flood ICS networks with fake requests, causing systems to crash or malfunction.

Common targets: OPC-UA, MQTT, PROFINET.

How to Secure Industrial Communication Protocols

Now that we know the threats, let's talk about how to stop them. Here's how to fortify your industrial networks and protocols against cyberattacks:

✓ 1. Implement Encryption & Authentication

🔒 **Use Secure Versions of Industrial Protocols**: Opt for TLS-encrypted versions of OPC-UA and MQTT. Avoid legacy Modbus and DNP3 when possible.
🔒 **Require Strong Authentication**: Implement device authentication to prevent unauthorized devices from sending commands.
🔒 **Use VPNs for Remote Access**: If remote monitoring is necessary, use a VPN with strong encryption to secure communication.

✓ 2. Network Segmentation & Zero Trust

Separate IT and OT networks: Keep industrial control systems isolated from the corporate network and internet.

Implement Firewalls & Access Control Lists (ACLs): Block unauthorized traffic from reaching critical devices.

Adopt Zero Trust Architecture (ZTA): Assume every connection is untrusted until verified.

✅ 3. Deploy Intrusion Detection Systems (IDS) for ICS

☐ Use network anomaly detection to identify suspicious traffic.

☐ Deploy ICS-specific IDS solutions (like Nozomi Networks, Dragos, or Claroty) that monitor industrial protocols for unusual activity.

☐ Set up alerts for unexpected commands or unauthorized data access.

✅ 4. Monitor & Log Everything

📊 Enable logging on all industrial devices to track unauthorized access attempts.

📊 Analyze network traffic for signs of MITM, injection, or replay attacks.

📊 Use Security Information and Event Management (SIEM) tools to correlate attack patterns.

✅ 5. Regularly Update & Patch ICS Firmware

☐ Keep all PLCs, RTUs, and SCADA software updated.

☐ Apply security patches as soon as they are released.

☐ Disable unnecessary protocols to reduce attack surfaces.

✅ 6. Implement Role-Based Access Control (RBAC)

🔑 Restrict who can access and modify ICS settings.

🔑 Require multi-factor authentication (MFA) for critical systems.

🔑 Limit remote access only to verified personnel.

Final Thoughts: Industrial Cybersecurity is NOT Optional

Let's be real—industrial systems are under attack like never before. Hackers are no longer just targeting IT networks—they're going after power grids, manufacturing plants, water treatment facilities, and oil refineries.

The good news? You can fight back.

Securing industrial communication protocols isn't just an IT task—it's a business-critical mission. If you run an ICS, SCADA, or IIoT environment, you have to assume that attackers are already trying to break in.

So lock down your protocols, encrypt your traffic, and never assume that legacy systems are safe just because they've been running for decades. The next cyberattack won't care how long your factory has been in business—it'll just look for the easiest way in. Don't let that be your network. 🚨

Chapter 8: Cyber-Physical Attacks and Smart Factory Exploits

Messing with cyber-physical systems isn't just about stealing data—it's about breaking things in the real world. Imagine manipulating an industrial robot to misassemble products, tampering with power grids, or causing temperature sensors in a chemical plant to report false readings. Welcome to the terrifying world of cyber-physical attacks, where digital exploits have real-world consequences.

This chapter covers cyber-physical security risks, including sabotage, side-channel attacks, and supply chain vulnerabilities. We'll examine the impact of malicious firmware modifications, sensor manipulation, and physical access exploits in IIoT environments, along with best practices for strengthening cyber-physical security.

8.1 Understanding Cyber-Physical Security Risks in IIoT

Welcome to the Wild, Wild (Cyber) West of Industrial IoT

Imagine this: You walk into a factory, and everything is digitally connected—robot arms assembling products, conveyor belts humming along, sensors monitoring temperature, humidity, and pressure. It's a technological marvel—until someone remotely hacks a PLC, cranks up the motor speed, and turns the entire operation into a multi-million-dollar fireworks show. ✸

This isn't a sci-fi movie. It's real-life cyber-physical risk in Industrial IoT (IIoT).

See, industrial environments aren't just about data breaches and stolen passwords. They involve real-world consequences—explosions, factory shutdowns, water contamination, power grid failures. In IIoT, a cyberattack isn't just about stealing data—it's about breaking things.

If hackers infiltrate your IT network, you might lose customer data. If they infiltrate your IIoT systems, you might lose an entire factory. Welcome to the high-stakes game of cyber-physical security. Let's break it down.

What is Cyber-Physical Security?

Cyber-physical security focuses on protecting industrial systems that have both digital and physical components. These are systems where cyberattacks can result in real-world physical damage.

Think of it like this:

IT Security → Protects data (emails, databases, passwords).

Cyber-Physical Security → Protects machines, infrastructure, and human safety.

Cyber-physical threats don't just come from traditional hacking techniques. They also involve:

● **Manipulating industrial processes** (e.g., altering chemical mixtures, tampering with factory automation).
● **Compromising safety systems** (e.g., disabling emergency shutdowns, overloading electrical circuits).
● **Attacking physical infrastructure** (e.g., disrupting power grids, sabotaging supply chains).

So, why is this such a big deal in IIoT? Because industrial systems are becoming more connected than ever.

The Growing Cyber-Physical Threat in IIoT

Once upon a time, industrial systems were air-gapped—meaning they weren't connected to the internet. If you wanted to mess with a power plant, you'd have to physically walk in and do it yourself.

Fast forward to today, and IIoT has changed everything. Factories, oil rigs, water treatment plants, and power grids are all connected, monitored, and controlled remotely. While this is great for efficiency, it's also a goldmine for cybercriminals.

Here's why:

● **Insecure Legacy Systems**: Many industrial systems were designed decades ago with no cybersecurity in mind.
● **Increased Connectivity**: SCADA, PLCs, and ICS are now exposed to the internet via remote access and cloud integration.

● **Lack of Cybersecurity Awareness**: Traditional OT engineers focus on keeping machines running, not stopping hackers.

Hackers love this situation. Why? Because they don't just get to steal information—they get to shut down production lines, disrupt cities, and cause chaos.

Common Cyber-Physical Security Risks in IIoT

1. Ransomware on Industrial Systems

Attackers encrypt critical control systems and demand ransom.

This has crippled factories, shut down pipelines, and halted manufacturing.

Example: The Colonial Pipeline ransomware attack (2021) caused fuel shortages across the U.S.

2. Sabotaging Industrial Processes

Hackers manipulate SCADA and PLC settings to cause machine failures.

Example: Changing chemical compositions in a water treatment plant (too much chlorine? Not enough? Both are dangerous).

3. Exploiting Wireless IIoT Devices

Attackers jam wireless sensor networks, causing automation failures.

Example: Disrupting warehouse robots by interfering with RFID and LoRa signals.

4. Attacking Safety Systems

Hackers disable emergency shutdown procedures, making industrial accidents worse.

Example: The Triton malware attack (2017) targeted industrial safety controllers at a petrochemical plant, trying to cause an explosion.

5. Power Grid Manipulation

Attackers infiltrate power SCADA systems, causing blackouts.

Example: The Ukraine power grid attack (2015) left 230,000 people in the dark.

These aren't hypothetical threats. These attacks have already happened—and they're becoming more frequent and sophisticated.

How to Protect Against Cyber-Physical Attacks

The good news? You don't have to be a sitting duck. Here's how to strengthen your IIoT infrastructure against cyber-physical threats.

✅ 1. Implement a Zero Trust Security Model

🚫 Assume that no device, user, or network traffic is safe—even inside your factory.
🔐 Require strict authentication and authorization for all IIoT devices.
☐ Limit access to industrial control systems—only approved personnel should have access.

✅ 2. Secure Industrial Networks with Segmentation

🔀 Separate IT and OT networks to prevent crossover attacks.
🔒 Use firewalls and VLANs to isolate critical IIoT devices.
☐ Deploy intrusion detection systems (IDS) to monitor traffic for suspicious activity.

✅ 3. Monitor and Log Everything

📊 Set up real-time monitoring of IIoT systems to detect anomalies.
💼 Log all access and changes to control systems.
☐ Use AI-based threat detection to catch unusual behavior before it escalates.

✅ 4. Regularly Patch and Update Firmware

☐ Keep all PLCs, RTUs, and SCADA software updated.
☐ Apply security patches as soon as they are available.
☐ Disable unused services and ports to reduce attack surfaces.

✅ 5. Conduct Red Team / Blue Team Exercises

🔥 Simulate real-world cyberattacks on your IIoT infrastructure.

☐ Train security teams on how to detect and respond to industrial cyber threats.

🎯 Test incident response plans to ensure quick recovery from attacks.

Final Thoughts: The Future of Cyber-Physical Security

Let's face it: IIoT security isn't optional anymore. The days of assuming "hackers only care about IT networks" are long gone. Attackers know that shutting down a factory, contaminating water supplies, or causing power outages is way more impactful than stealing some emails.

So, what's the takeaway?

🖥 If you're working in an industrial environment, you need to start thinking like a hacker.

That means:

✅ Locking down your industrial networks.

✅ Hardening IIoT devices against cyber threats.

✅ Training your teams to detect and respond to cyber-physical attacks.

The next cyberattack isn't going to wait for you to be ready. So start securing your IIoT systems today—before someone else does it for you (the hard way). 💀

8.2 Sabotaging Industrial Processes Through Cyber Attacks

Welcome to the Dark Side of Industrial Hacking

Imagine you're the proud operator of a high-tech manufacturing plant, where robotic arms dance in perfect harmony, conveyor belts hum with precision, and production runs smoother than your morning coffee. Then—BAM!—the robotic arms start smashing into each other like a bar fight gone wrong, the conveyor belts speed up to NASCAR levels, and your carefully manufactured products now resemble modern art sculptures.

What happened? You've just been digitally sabotaged.

Cybercriminals aren't just after data anymore. They're attacking industrial processes, manipulating machinery, and causing real-world destruction. This isn't some Hollywood hacker fantasy—this is happening right now, in factories, power plants, water treatment facilities, and beyond. And if you think this can't happen to your industrial control system (ICS), think again.

Now, let's dive into how cyberattacks can sabotage industrial processes, why they work, and—most importantly—how you can prevent your factory from becoming the next cautionary tale.

How Do Cyberattacks Sabotage Industrial Processes?

Industrial sabotage used to require a wrench, a crowbar, and some really bad intentions. Today? A laptop and an internet connection are all you need.

Industrial IoT (IIoT) and SCADA (Supervisory Control and Data Acquisition) systems control critical infrastructure—power grids, water plants, chemical refineries, oil pipelines, and manufacturing plants. These systems were designed to prioritize availability and efficiency, not cybersecurity. And hackers know it.

Here's how they can digitally sabotage industrial processes:

1. Manipulating Setpoints and Sensor Data

📊 Hackers alter readings from industrial sensors (temperature, pressure, flow rate) to trick operators into making wrong decisions.
🔥 **Example**: Increasing the reported temperature in a cooling system, forcing an unnecessary shutdown.

2. Overloading or Disabling Safety Mechanisms

☐ Attackers disable emergency shutdown systems, making it impossible to stop runaway processes.
✸ **Example**: Triton Malware (2017) attempted to disable safety systems in a petrochemical plant, risking an explosion.

3. Increasing Machine Speeds Beyond Safe Limits

⚙ Hackers remotely tweak PLC settings to crank up motor speeds, causing equipment failures or even physical destruction.
🔧 **Example**: A centrifuge running at hyper-speed until it self-destructs (sounds familiar? Cough Stuxnet cough).

4. Tampering with Chemical Mixtures

☣ Industrial processes rely on precise chemical compositions. Attackers can alter mix ratios, turning everyday operations into biohazards.
🏭 **Example**: Contaminating a water treatment plant's chemical dosing system, leading to unsafe drinking water.

5. Power Grid Manipulation & Blackouts

⚡ Hackers infiltrate power SCADA systems, remotely switching breakers on and off, causing widespread power failures.
💡 **Example**: Ukraine Power Grid Attack (2015) left 230,000 people without electricity after hackers remotely flipped switches.

These attacks aren't just hypothetical—they're real, growing, and dangerous.

Real-World Cyber Sabotage: Stuxnet and Beyond

If you've ever heard the term "cyber warfare," then you've heard of Stuxnet—the world's first digital weapon that sabotaged an industrial process.

Case Study: Stuxnet (2010) – A Blueprint for Cyber Sabotage

◆ Stuxnet was a highly sophisticated worm that targeted Iran's nuclear enrichment facilities.
◆ It manipulated Siemens PLCs, making centrifuges spin too fast and then slow down, causing physical degradation.
◆ The malware fed false data to monitoring systems, so operators saw everything as normal—until machines started breaking down.
◆ 1,000+ centrifuges were destroyed—without a single bomb being dropped.

Stuxnet was only the beginning.

Since then, we've seen:

Triton (2017): Targeted safety systems in petrochemical plants.

BlackEnergy (2015): Took down Ukraine's power grid.

Industroyer (2016): Disrupted European power networks.

Oldsmar Water Plant Attack (2021): A hacker increased lye levels in a Florida water plant to dangerous levels.

These aren't prank hacks. These are strategic, calculated attacks designed to disrupt industries, damage economies, and threaten human safety.

Defending Against Industrial Process Sabotage

The good news? You can fight back. Here's how.

✅ 1. Implement Strong Network Segmentation

☐ Separate IT and OT networks so hackers can't hop from corporate email servers to industrial control systems.
🚫 Air-gap critical systems that don't need internet access.
🔒 Use firewalls and intrusion detection for monitoring.

✅ 2. Secure PLCs and SCADA Systems

🔐 Change default passwords on all industrial controllers.
☐ Keep firmware updated and patch known vulnerabilities.
📲 Use multi-factor authentication (MFA) for remote access.

✅ 3. Implement Real-Time Monitoring and Anomaly Detection

👀 Deploy ICS-specific threat detection solutions to spot unusual activity.
📉 Set up real-time alerts for changes in PLC configurations.
☐ Use AI-powered monitoring tools to detect abnormal behavior in industrial processes.

✅ 4. Train OT Engineers in Cybersecurity

🎓 Most OT (Operational Technology) engineers focus on keeping machines running, not stopping hackers. Change that.

👤♦️ Conduct red team/blue team exercises in industrial environments.

🔍 Teach operators how to spot suspicious behavior on HMIs and SCADA systems.

✅ 5. Develop an Incident Response Plan for Industrial Cyber Attacks

🚨 Create a playbook for handling ICS breaches.

🔥 Test emergency shutdown procedures to ensure they work under cyberattack conditions.

📞 Maintain offline backups of critical configurations in case of ransomware.

Final Thoughts: Cyber Sabotage is the New Industrial Warfare

Forget spy movies and Hollywood hacking scenes—industrial cyber sabotage is already here.

If your factory, power plant, or water treatment facility relies on IIoT, SCADA, or PLC-based automation, you need to assume hackers are watching. The real question is:

Are you prepared to stop them?

🔒 Lock down your IIoT systems.

⚡ Secure your SCADA and PLCs.

🎯 Train your teams to detect and respond to industrial cyber threats.

Because the next cyberattack won't just steal your data—it might shut down your entire operation.

Stay vigilant, stay secure, and for the love of all things industrial—don't let a hacker turn your factory into an explosive case study. 🚀🔥

8.3 Exploiting Physical Access to Smart Factory Systems

Breaking In: The Cyberpunk Heist You Didn't See Coming

Picture this: You're a hacker, dressed like an unsuspecting maintenance worker, strolling into a smart factory. Security is tight—at least digitally. Firewalls, VPNs, multi-factor authentication. But here's the kicker: the IT team forgot about one tiny, gaping hole in their security plan—physical access.

You walk over to a control cabinet, open it with a generic industrial key (which, by the way, you bought online for $10), and plug in a tiny rogue device. Congratulations! You now have a foothold into the factory's internal network. Who needs to crack a firewall when you can literally walk up to a PLC and hack it from the inside?

While most cybersecurity defenses focus on stopping remote attackers, a shocking number of breaches start with someone physically tampering with hardware. And in the world of Industrial IoT (IIoT), physical security is just as important as digital security.

Let's dive into how attackers exploit physical access in smart factories—and how you can lock them out before they turn your facility into a hacker's playground.

Why Physical Access is a Major Security Risk in IIoT

Industrial facilities are big, complex, and full of connected devices—from PLCs and HMIs to network switches and RFID readers. Many of these systems were designed with availability in mind, not security.

Unlike IT environments where servers sit safely behind locked doors, industrial control devices are often out in the open, inside control rooms, factory floors, or even remote substations. If an attacker can physically touch a device, they can potentially own it.

What makes physical access so dangerous?

Direct hardware manipulation – Attackers can modify PLCs, sabotage safety mechanisms, or even install hardware trojans.

Unauthorized USB & network access – A single rogue USB drive or network drop can grant attackers full control.

Tampering with badge or biometric authentication – If an attacker can clone an access card, they can walk right in.

Plant-floor social engineering – If someone looks like they belong (contractors, vendors, or employees), security is often relaxed.

In short: If an attacker can touch it, they can hack it.

Physical Attack Vectors in Smart Factories

Let's break down some of the most common ways attackers exploit physical access in industrial environments.

1. USB Drops: Malware on a Stick

👀 Ever found a random USB drive lying around? Hackers hope you'll plug it in out of curiosity.

☠ **Example**: Stuxnet spread via infected USB drives, taking down Iran's nuclear centrifuges.

🔒 **Prevention**: Disable USB ports on critical systems and use data diode solutions for secure file transfers.

2. Rogue Devices: The Evil Twin of Industrial Networks

💻 Attackers plant rogue Raspberry Pi, Wi-Fi Pineapple, or keyloggers inside a factory.

🔌 **Example**: A hacker plugs in a small computer inside a network cabinet, gaining remote access.

🔒 **Prevention**: Monitor and inspect all physical connections—especially inside control cabinets.

3. Badge Cloning & Tailgating: Walking Right In

🪪 Many smart factories rely on RFID badges for access control—but cloning these is child's play.

🚪 **Example**: An attacker follows an employee through a security door (tailgating) or uses a cloned badge.

🔒 **Prevention**: Implement multi-factor authentication (MFA) for secure access.

4. Tampering with PLCs & Industrial Controllers

⚙️ If an attacker has physical access to a PLC, RTU, or industrial controller, they can:

Change process setpoints (causing unsafe conditions).

Inject malicious firmware (creating persistent backdoors).

Erase logs to cover tracks.

🔒 **Prevention**: Lock control cabinets, disable unused ports, and monitor physical access logs.

5. Exploiting Remote Access Points & HMI Terminals

🖥 Many smart factories have HMI terminals (Human-Machine Interfaces) in open areas.
💀 If an attacker walks up and finds an unlocked session, they can control the entire process.
🔒 **Prevention**: Auto-lock terminals and enforce strict access control policies.

Real-World Case Studies: When Physical Access Led to Disaster

Case #1: Maroochy Water Plant Hack (2000)

🔑 A disgruntled ex-employee used stolen SCADA credentials to release 264,000 gallons of raw sewage into waterways.
💀 **How**? He had physical access to SCADA control systems before being fired and knew exactly how to manipulate them.
🔒 **Lesson**: Revoke access immediately for ex-employees, and log all physical interactions with control systems.

Case #2: Ukraine Power Grid Attack (2015)

⚡ Russian hackers used a combination of phishing & physical access to disrupt Ukraine's power grid.
💀 The attack shut down 30 substations, leaving 230,000 people without electricity.
🔒 **Lesson**: Secure industrial substations, and don't rely solely on software-based security.

Defending Against Physical Attacks in Smart Factories

So, how do you stop an attacker from literally walking into your factory and wreaking havoc?

✅ 1. Implement Strict Access Controls

🔐 Use multi-factor authentication (MFA) for all critical systems.

☐ Implement role-based access control (RBAC)—not everyone needs access to everything.

📷 Deploy surveillance cameras and monitor physical entry points.

✅ 2. Lock Down Physical Ports and Control Cabinets

☐☐ Lock cabinets containing PLCs, RTUs, and network switches.

🔌 Disable unused USB ports and Ethernet jacks to prevent rogue device insertion.

🏷 Consider tamper-evident seals to detect unauthorized access.

✅ 3. Train Employees to Spot Social Engineering

☐👥 Conduct security awareness training for all factory workers.

🎭 Teach staff to challenge "fake contractors" or "suspicious technicians".

🔒 Use visitor escort policies—don't let strangers roam freely.

✅ 4. Deploy Intrusion Detection Systems (IDS) for Physical Security

🏷 Use RFID tracking for employees & contractors.

☐ Install motion sensors & security cameras in sensitive areas.

🖬 Maintain logs of all physical and digital access attempts.

✅ 5. Conduct Regular Security Audits & Red Team Exercises

💻 Hire ethical hackers (red teams) to test your physical security defenses.

🏢 Perform regular site security audits to find vulnerabilities before attackers do.

🔍 Test real-world attack scenarios (like USB drops & badge cloning).

Final Thoughts: The Key to Security is Keeping Hackers OUT

At the end of the day, your factory is only as secure as its weakest point—and sometimes, that weak point isn't a fancy firewall or a zero-day exploit. It's a door left open.

If attackers can physically access your IIoT devices, it's game over. So, treat physical security as seriously as you do network security.

Because the last thing you want is a hacker in disguise waltzing into your factory and turning your million-dollar smart system into a very expensive paperweight. 🚀▯

8.4 Side-Channel and Power Analysis Attacks on IIoT Devices

Hacking Without Hacking: The Sneaky Art of Side-Channel Attacks

Picture this: You're in a high-stakes cyber showdown, hacking into an Industrial IoT (IIoT) system. Firewalls? Unbreakable. Encryption? Solid. Multi-factor authentication? Annoyingly robust. But what if I told you that you could steal secrets from a device without ever breaking its encryption, guessing a password, or even touching the network?

Welcome to the James Bond-level cyber heist known as side-channel attacks. Instead of breaking the cryptography itself, attackers eavesdrop on the physical side effects of a system: power consumption, electromagnetic emissions, timing variations, even the tiny sounds a CPU makes while processing. It's hacking without hacking—like stealing someone's ATM PIN by watching how their fingers move on the keypad.

For industrial environments, where IIoT devices control everything from assembly lines to power grids, this is a serious problem. Attackers don't need root access if they can just listen in on how a system processes data and extract encryption keys, authentication tokens, or control signals passively.

Sounds like sci-fi? Think again. Let's break it down.

What Are Side-Channel Attacks?

At its core, a side-channel attack is when a hacker exploits leaked physical information from a device instead of breaking its software security. Think of it like cracking a safe by listening to the clicking sounds of the lock instead of brute-forcing the combination.

Common side-channel attack techniques include:

Power Analysis Attacks – Measuring power consumption patterns to extract cryptographic keys.

Electromagnetic (EM) Attacks – Capturing electromagnetic radiation from a device to reconstruct sensitive data.

Timing Attacks – Observing how long operations take to infer data processing steps.

Acoustic Attacks – Analyzing subtle sounds produced by electronic components.

Thermal Attacks – Examining heat signatures to predict recent computational activity.

These techniques are particularly dangerous for low-power IIoT devices, SCADA systems, and industrial controllers, which often lack strong defenses against physical observation.

Power Analysis Attacks: The Low-Key Threat to IIoT Security

Every electronic device draws power in a unique way, and an attacker can use this information to reconstruct secret data.

1. Simple Power Analysis (SPA)

Attackers analyze basic power consumption patterns to determine operations being executed.

Example: If a smart meter draws more power when encrypting vs. when idle, an attacker can identify when encryption keys are being used.

2. Differential Power Analysis (DPA)

More advanced: Attackers collect power consumption data over multiple executions and use statistical techniques to extract cryptographic keys.

Example: If a SCADA system uses AES encryption, an attacker could correlate power usage with encryption rounds to reveal the AES key.

🔒 **Defensive Measures:**

✓ Use power-randomization techniques to introduce noise into power consumption.

✓☐ Implement constant power draw circuits to prevent analysis.
✓☐ Design hardware to limit external power leakage.

Electromagnetic (EM) Attacks: Stealing Data Through the Air

Every electronic device emits electromagnetic radiation—it's a natural byproduct of electricity flowing through circuits. But here's the scary part: attackers can capture these emissions and reconstruct the data being processed.

Real-World EM Attack Example:

☐☐♂☐ In 2015, researchers demonstrated how they could extract encryption keys from a laptop just by placing an antenna near it—all using radio waves!

In an IIoT environment, this means:

Attackers could wirelessly eavesdrop on smart meters, industrial controllers, or PLCs.

Critical data (like authentication tokens or sensor readings) could be extracted remotely.

Even if a system is air-gapped, EM emissions can be sniffed from outside the facility.

🔒 Defensive Measures:

✓☐ Use shielded enclosures (Faraday cages) for sensitive equipment.
✓☐ Implement EM noise generators to mask emissions.
✓☐ Conduct EM leakage testing during device design.

Timing Attacks: When Milliseconds Matter

Sometimes, just measuring how long an operation takes can reveal secrets.
For example:

If a login system processes incorrect passwords faster than correct ones, an attacker can infer valid credentials.

If an industrial controller takes slightly longer to process certain commands, an attacker could predict when encryption is being used.

📻 Dangerous IIoT Timing Attack Example:

Imagine a hacker sending thousands of fake authentication requests to a factory's access control system. By analyzing response times, they can slowly reconstruct valid passwords—without ever brute-forcing them.

🔒 Defensive Measures:

✓☐ Use constant-time execution for authentication and encryption functions.
✓☐ Add random delays in system responses.
✓☐ Implement rate limiting to prevent rapid-fire timing attacks.

Acoustic & Thermal Attacks: The Unexpected Threats

Yeah, you read that right—hackers can steal data based on sound and heat.

🎧 Acoustic Attacks:

Keyboards, CPUs, and even industrial PLCs emit subtle sounds when operating.

An attacker with a microphone can record these sounds and use AI to reconstruct data.

Example: A smart factory's robotic arm produces slightly different sounds when following different programmed paths—a hacker could "listen" to steal the production sequence.

🔥 Thermal Attacks:

Devices heat up differently depending on the data they process.

Thermal cameras or heat-sensitive trojans can reveal past computational activity.

Example: An attacker places a thermal sensor on a PLC, waits for it to execute commands, and later retrieves heat signatures to infer operational data.

🔒 Defensive Measures:

✓☐ Use thermal insulation and sound-dampening techniques.
✓☐ Encrypt even low-level operations to prevent data inference.
✓☐ Introduce random execution noise to prevent pattern recognition.

Final Thoughts: How to Stop Side-Channel Attacks in IIoT

🔐 Unlike traditional cyberattacks, side-channel attacks are nearly impossible to detect with software-based security tools. That means firewalls, intrusion detection systems, and encryption alone aren't enough.

Key Takeaways for IIoT Security:

✅ **Harden hardware** – Design IIoT devices to resist power analysis, EM leakage, and timing attacks.
✅ **Shield critical components** – Use Faraday cages and physical shielding to block unwanted emissions.
✅ **Randomize execution patterns** – Prevent timing and power-based attacks with noise and unpredictability.
✅ **Monitor for rogue devices** – Attackers may plant listening devices near IIoT systems to capture emissions.

The Bottom Line?

Attackers don't always hack software—sometimes, they just listen to how a system operates and steal secrets without breaking a single line of code. So if you're serious about IIoT security, don't just think in ones and zeros—think about power, timing, sound, and even heat.

Otherwise, the next time your factory mysteriously shuts down, you'll be left wondering… was it a cyberattack, or just a really smart eavesdropper? 😼 🔌

8.5 Strengthening Cyber-Physical Security in Industrial Environments

Cyber-Physical Security: Because Hackers Don't Just Stay in Cyberspace

Let's be honest—most people think of hackers as hoodie-wearing keyboard warriors, sipping energy drinks and launching attacks from a dimly lit basement. But in the world of Industrial IoT (IIoT), attackers don't just live in the digital realm. They cut wires, plant rogue devices, manipulate sensors, and even walk into facilities pretending to be maintenance workers.

That's right—cyber-physical attacks are a whole different game. In this world, hacking isn't just about firewalls and malware; it's about tampering with industrial robots, disrupting manufacturing lines, and making smart factories go haywire. Imagine an attacker subtly altering temperature sensors in a chemical plant or tricking an automated warehouse system into misplacing inventory. The consequences? Financial losses, safety risks, and potential industrial disasters.

So how do we keep bad actors out of both our networks and our physical spaces? Welcome to the cyber-physical security battleground.

Understanding Cyber-Physical Security in IIoT

Cyber-physical security is all about protecting systems that bridge the digital and physical worlds. In industrial environments, these systems include:

✓ **Programmable Logic Controllers (PLCs)** – The "brains" of factory automation.
✓ **Supervisory Control and Data Acquisition (SCADA) systems** – The digital overseers of industrial operations.
✓ **Smart sensors and actuators** – Devices that measure and control real-world processes.
✓ **Industrial robots and automated machinery** – The backbone of modern manufacturing.

Because these systems interact with both software and physical processes, they face hybrid attack scenarios where hackers exploit both digital weaknesses and real-world vulnerabilities.

What Makes Cyber-Physical Attacks So Dangerous?

They're Hard to Detect – If malware slows down a production line, is it a cyberattack or just mechanical failure?

They Can Cause Physical Damage – A rogue command to a factory robot can lead to equipment damage or even human injury.

They Combine Digital and Physical Intrusions – An attacker can physically manipulate an industrial system without ever touching the network.

Let's dive into real-world cyber-physical attack tactics and, more importantly, how to stop them.

1. Preventing Unauthorized Physical Access

Attackers love weak physical security. If they can walk into a facility unnoticed, they can:

◆ Install rogue devices (e.g., Raspberry Pis, Wi-Fi sniffers) inside a factory.
◆ Tamper with sensors and PLCs to create operational disruptions.
◆ Steal authentication credentials from unattended workstations.

🔒 How to Defend Against Physical Intrusions:

✓ **Strict access control** – Use biometric locks, smart ID cards, and multi-factor authentication at all entry points.
✓ **Surveillance & monitoring** – Deploy CCTV cameras, motion sensors, and AI-powered anomaly detection.
✓ **Security drills & employee training** – Teach staff to recognize social engineering attacks (e.g., tailgating, fake maintenance workers).

🚨 Case Study: The "Janitor Hack"

A hacker once dressed as a janitor, entered an industrial facility, and installed a tiny malware-infected USB device into a workstation. The malware spread through the factory network, causing production slowdowns. Moral of the story? Even janitors need security clearance.

2. Securing Industrial Networks from Cyber-Physical Manipulation

Even if attackers can't physically access your factory, they can still remotely tamper with industrial processes.

Common Tactics Used by Cyber-Physical Attackers:

◆ **Sensor Spoofing** – Manipulating temperature, pressure, or motion sensors to feed false data into control systems.
◆ **Remote Command Injection** – Hijacking a PLC to send rogue commands (e.g., shutting down production).

◆ **Firmware Tampering** – Modifying firmware in IIoT devices to introduce hidden backdoors.

🔒 **How to Defend Against Digital Cyber-Physical Attacks:**

✔ **Network segmentation** – Isolate OT (Operational Technology) networks from IT networks to prevent lateral movement.

✔ **Real-time monitoring** – Use anomaly detection systems to flag suspicious command executions.

✔ **Authenticated firmware updates** – Implement cryptographically signed firmware to prevent unauthorized modifications.

✔ **Red Team Testing** – Simulate cyber-physical attacks to test factory defenses against real-world threats.

🔍 **Case Study: Stuxnet – The Ultimate Cyber-Physical Attack**

The infamous Stuxnet worm didn't steal data—it sabotaged Iranian nuclear centrifuges by secretly altering their operational speeds. The attack remained undetected for months because everything looked normal in software, but the physical equipment was being destroyed.

3. Protecting Industrial Robots and Automated Systems

Industrial robots are awesome, but they also introduce huge security risks. Attackers can:

◆ Reprogram robots to sabotage manufacturing processes.
◆ Use network attacks to remotely control smart machinery.
◆ Exploit unpatched firmware to introduce hidden vulnerabilities.

🔒 **How to Defend Industrial Robots from Cyber-Physical Threats:**

✔ **Secure robot control interfaces** – Limit access to only authorized personnel.

✔ **Implement behavior anomaly detection** – Use AI to detect abnormal robot movement patterns.

✔ **Encrypt robot communication protocols** – Prevent attackers from injecting rogue commands.

🔍 **Case Study: Robot Arm Hack**

Researchers demonstrated how an unsecured industrial robot arm could be remotely hacked to misplace parts in an assembly line—leading to defective products and massive financial losses.

4. Securing Smart Sensors and Actuators

IIoT sensors are small but critical. Attackers can:

◆ Tamper with environmental sensors to disrupt production conditions.
◆ Exploit unencrypted sensor data to feed false readings into SCADA systems.
◆ Overload actuators to cause mechanical failures.

🔒 How to Defend Smart Sensors and Actuators:

✓ Use encrypted communication for sensor data transmission.

✓ Calibrate sensors regularly to detect unauthorized tampering.

✓ Employ redundant sensor verification (i.e., compare multiple sensor readings to detect anomalies).

📷 Case Study: Smart Thermostat Attack

A hacker remotely altered a factory's smart thermostats, causing temperature-sensitive production processes to fail. The company lost millions before they even realized they were hacked.

Final Thoughts: Strengthening Cyber-Physical Security is Non-Negotiable

In IIoT environments, you're not just protecting data—you're protecting physical assets, operations, and human lives. A breach doesn't just mean stolen credentials or data leaks; it means sabotaged production lines, damaged equipment, and even safety hazards.

Key Takeaways:

✓☐ Physical security is just as important as cybersecurity.
✓☐ IIoT devices, sensors, and robots are all attack targets.
✓☐ Real-time anomaly detection is critical for cyber-physical security.

✓☐ Encryption, segmentation, and firmware security should be standard.

The Bottom Line? If you're securing an industrial environment, think beyond firewalls and passwords. The next attack might not come through a phishing email—it could come from a tampered sensor, a hacked robot, or a fake maintenance worker with a USB stick.

So lock those doors, secure your networks, and maybe… double-check if that janitor is really supposed to be there. 🌐🔒💡

Chapter 9: Incident Response and Threat Detection in IIoT

Alright, so the factory's under attack—alarms blaring, machines acting possessed, and the IT team is frantically Googling "How to stop ransomware in SCADA." Not exactly the ideal situation, huh? Unfortunately, many industrial organizations have no real incident response plan, which means they're stuck in panic mode when something goes wrong. But fear not! With real-time monitoring, anomaly detection, and a solid IR strategy, you can turn a full-blown cyber meltdown into just another day at the office.

This chapter explores incident response strategies and threat detection methodologies for IIoT environments. We'll cover real-time monitoring, behavioral anomaly detection, and forensic analysis techniques tailored for industrial networks. Additionally, we'll discuss how AI and machine learning can enhance IIoT threat intelligence and help organizations build a cyber-resilient infrastructure.

9.1 Implementing Real-Time Monitoring and Threat Intelligence for ICS

Why Catching Cyberattacks in Real Time is Like Spotting a Ninja in the Dark

Imagine this: You're running a high-tech smart factory, everything is automated, humming along smoothly, and then—BAM!—a production line mysteriously slows down, temperature sensors start reporting false readings, and your SCADA system locks you out.

Congratulations! You're either experiencing a massive cyberattack, or your factory AI has decided to rebel and start its own industrial revolution. Either way, you didn't see it coming, and that's a problem.

This is why real-time monitoring and threat intelligence for Industrial Control Systems (ICS) is critical. Unlike traditional IT systems, ICS environments control physical processes—meaning a cyberattack isn't just about data theft; it can shut down entire factories, wreck supply chains, and even put human lives at risk.

So, how do we go from being blind to cyber threats to spotting and stopping attacks in real time? Let's dive in.

Understanding Real-Time Monitoring in ICS

What is Real-Time Monitoring?

Real-time monitoring is like having security cameras for your industrial network, constantly watching for suspicious activity, unusual patterns, and potential threats before they escalate.

In an ICS environment, this means continuously analyzing:

🔍 **Network Traffic** – Is someone suddenly accessing PLCs they shouldn't?

🔍 **System Logs** – Any strange login attempts or unauthorized changes?

🔍 **Operational Data** – Are production parameters suddenly off?

🔍 **Endpoint Activity** – Any rogue devices connecting to your network?

Real-time monitoring allows security teams to detect threats the moment they happen, instead of discovering months later that an attacker has been lurking inside the network.

Key Benefits of Real-Time ICS Monitoring:

✓ **Instant Threat Detection** – Spot and respond to attacks before damage occurs.

✓ **Anomaly Detection** – Identify suspicious deviations in industrial processes.

✓ **Minimized Downtime** – Prevent cyber incidents from disrupting operations.

✓ **Regulatory Compliance** – Many industrial security standards require real-time monitoring (like NERC CIP, IEC 62443).

The Role of Threat Intelligence in ICS Security

What is Threat Intelligence?

Threat intelligence is like having an early warning system for cyberattacks. It helps security teams:

🔍 **Predict Attacks** – Identify new cyber threats targeting industrial systems.

🔍 **Understand Attack Tactics** – Learn how hackers exploit ICS vulnerabilities.

🔍 **Respond Faster** – Use up-to-date intelligence to react to emerging threats.

There are three main types of threat intelligence:

Strategic Intelligence – High-level insights into industry-wide threats and trends.

Tactical Intelligence – Information about specific attacker tactics and techniques.

Operational Intelligence – Real-time indicators of compromise (IOCs) to detect attacks as they happen.

Why ICS Threat Intelligence is Different from IT Threat Intelligence

- 💡 In IT, threat intelligence focuses on malware, phishing, and ransomware.
- 💡 In ICS, it includes physical disruptions, process manipulation, and protocol attacks.

For example, IT security might track ransomware gangs, while ICS threat intelligence focuses on attack groups like Xenotime (TRITON malware) that target industrial safety systems.

How to Implement Real-Time Monitoring & Threat Intelligence in ICS

Step 1: Deploy Industrial Intrusion Detection Systems (IDS/IPS)

- ◆ Use ICS-specific IDS/IPS solutions like Nozomi Networks, Dragos, or Claroty.
- ◆ Monitor SCADA traffic for suspicious commands.
- ◆ Set up automated alerts for unauthorized access to PLCs, RTUs, and HMIs.

🖥 **Example**: A power plant's ICS IDS detected a sudden flood of Modbus traffic—it turned out to be an attacker attempting a denial-of-service (DoS) attack on control systems.

Step 2: Use AI-Powered Anomaly Detection

✍ Traditional security tools look for known threats, but AI-powered systems detect unknown attacks by learning what "normal" industrial behavior looks like.

- ◆ Deploy machine learning-based anomaly detection tools.
- ◆ Identify out-of-pattern activity (e.g., a sudden spike in SCADA commands at 3 AM).
- ◆ Automatically block or isolate suspicious traffic in real time.

Example: An AI-based system at a water treatment plant flagged an unusual increase in chlorine levels—it turned out a hacker had remotely altered the chemical dosing system!

Step 3: Integrate Threat Intelligence Feeds

◆ Subscribe to ICS threat intelligence platforms like:

✓ MITRE ATT&CK for ICS

✓ Dragos Threat Intelligence

✓ US-CERT ICS Advisories

✓ Shodan & Censys for exposed ICS devices

◆ Automatically ingest threat intelligence feeds into SIEM (Security Information and Event Management) tools.

◆ Use Threat Hunting to proactively search for indicators of compromise (IOCs).

Example: A factory using threat intelligence feeds detected an IP linked to Russian APT groups scanning their network—allowing them to block the intrusion before an attack happened.

Step 4: Implement Automated Incident Response

🚀 When an attack happens, you don't have time to manually investigate—your response needs to be fast and automated.

◆ Use Security Orchestration, Automation, and Response (SOAR) platforms.

◆ Automate responses to ICS-specific threats (e.g., isolate compromised PLCs).

◆ Create playbooks for industrial cyber incidents.

Example: A pharmaceutical factory experienced an attack where an attacker tried to change drug formulation parameters—automated monitoring shut down the affected PLC before damage was done.

Step 5: Train Staff on ICS Threat Awareness

◆ Conduct regular cybersecurity drills simulating ICS-specific attacks.

- ◆ Train OT engineers on real-time monitoring tools and threat hunting techniques.
- ◆ Create incident response teams specializing in ICS cyber threats.

📟 **Example**: A factory conducted a "red team vs. blue team" exercise, simulating a SCADA attack—this helped engineers improve their real-time threat response skills.

Final Thoughts: Stay One Step Ahead of Attackers

Here's the deal: Cyber threats against ICS environments are only increasing. Attackers are getting smarter, using AI, and even selling ICS exploits on the dark web.

If you don't have real-time monitoring and threat intelligence, you're basically flying blind—and by the time you realize you've been hacked, it might be too late.

Key Takeaways:

✓☐ ICS monitoring is not optional—it's essential.
✓☐ AI-based anomaly detection helps catch unknown attacks.
✓☐ Threat intelligence keeps you ahead of cybercriminals.
✓☐ Automated responses minimize downtime.
✓☐ Training is just as important as technology.

Bottom Line? Invest in real-time ICS security, or be prepared to watch your smart factory turn into a very expensive paperweight. 📟 🔍

9.2 Detecting Anomalies and Behavioral Attacks in Industrial Networks

When Your Factory Starts Acting "Possessed"

Alright, picture this: You walk into your smart factory on a Monday morning, coffee in hand, ready to start the week. But something feels... off. The robotic arms are moving erratically, conveyor belts are speeding up and slowing down randomly, and your SCADA system is displaying temperatures that don't make sense.

Either your industrial network has been possessed by a cyber poltergeist, or you're dealing with a behavioral cyberattack. And trust me, the second option is much scarier.

Hackers have gotten smarter. Instead of launching brute-force attacks or dropping obvious malware, they're now subtly manipulating industrial processes to avoid detection while causing massive damage.

How do you catch an attacker who isn't triggering alarms but is slowly corrupting your entire operation? The answer: Anomaly detection and behavioral analysis. Let's break it down.

What is Anomaly Detection in Industrial Networks?

Defining "Normal" vs. "Suspicious" Behavior

In cybersecurity, an anomaly is anything that deviates from the expected behavior.

For example, in an industrial network:

✅ Normal Activity

A PLC sending temperature data every 5 seconds.

An operator logging into the SCADA system during work hours.

A robotic arm following a programmed routine.

🚨 Suspicious Activity (Anomalies)

A PLC suddenly sending data every 1 second instead of every 5.

An operator logging in at 3 AM from an unknown location.

A robotic arm executing unauthorized movements.

By continuously monitoring network traffic, user behavior, and system commands, anomaly detection tools can identify when something unusual is happening, even if it doesn't match a known cyberattack pattern.

Common Behavioral Attacks in ICS Networks

1. Slow and Subtle Process Manipulation

Instead of shutting down a factory in one big attack, hackers may gradually manipulate process variables to cause slow damage.

✦ **Example**: A hacker increases the temperature in an oil refinery by 0.1°C per hour—small enough to go unnoticed, but after a few weeks, equipment overheats and fails.

☐ **Detection Method**: Monitor for long-term trends and deviations in process variables.

2. Masquerading as a Legitimate User

Instead of brute-forcing passwords, attackers may steal login credentials and blend in as a regular operator.

✦ **Example**: A hacker gains access to an engineer's account and issues malicious SCADA commands that appear to be normal activity.

☐ **Detection Method**: Use behavioral analytics to flag logins from unusual locations or times.

3. Time-Based Attacks

Some attacks are programmed to activate at specific times, making them harder to detect in real-time.

✦ **Example**: A compromised PLC remains dormant for months and then suddenly executes a rogue command at midnight to sabotage production.

☐ **Detection Method**: Use historical data analysis to identify devices that are behaving differently than before.

4. Man-in-the-Middle (MITM) on Industrial Protocols

Attackers can intercept and alter SCADA commands without detection.

✦ **Example**: A hacker modifies sensor data so that the system believes pressure levels are normal—even when they're dangerously high.

☐ **Detection Method**: Implement deep packet inspection (DPI) to analyze ICS protocol traffic for unusual modifications.

How to Detect Behavioral Attacks and Anomalies in Industrial Networks

1. Implement AI-Powered Anomaly Detection Systems

Traditional cybersecurity tools rely on signatures of known attacks. But AI-powered anomaly detection can spot new, unknown threats by learning what "normal" network behavior looks like.

⬥ **Solution**: Use AI-based anomaly detection platforms like:

Darktrace for Industrial Networks

Nozomi Networks Guardian

Dragos Threat Detection

🔎 **Example**: A smart grid system detected an unusual pattern in energy consumption—it turned out to be a hacker secretly manipulating power distribution.

2. Use Behavioral Analytics on Users & Devices

Instead of just logging user activity, analyze their behavior over time.

⬥ **Solution**: Deploy User and Entity Behavior Analytics (UEBA) to detect:

✓ Logins from unusual locations
✓ Operators accessing systems they've never used before
✓ PLCs issuing unexpected commands

🔎 **Example**: A factory detected an operator logging in from Russia—but the operator was on vacation in the U.S.. This led to catching a credential theft attack in progress.

3. Correlate Data Across Multiple Sources

◆ **Don't just monitor network logs—combine data from:**

✓ SCADA logs

✅ Firewall logs

✅ Industrial sensors

✅ User authentication logs

🔊 **Example**: A steel plant correlated process logs with network logs and found a rogue device issuing commands to industrial robots.

4. Set Up Honeytokens in ICS Systems

Honeytokens are fake credentials, fake data, or decoy devices that trick attackers into revealing themselves.

◆ **Solution**: Deploy fake PLCs, fake logins, or fake Modbus registers.

🔊 **Example**: A water treatment facility set up a fake SCADA login page—when an attacker tried to access it, security teams instantly detected and blocked them.

5. Use Threat Intelligence Feeds for ICS

◆ Subscribe to ICS-specific threat intelligence feeds to stay ahead of emerging threats.

✅ MITRE ATT&CK for ICS

✅ Dragos Threat Intelligence

✅ ICS-CERT Alerts

🔊 **Example**: A factory detected a known IP address linked to an ICS malware campaign—preventing an attack before it started.

Final Thoughts: Stay One Step Ahead

If you're waiting for alarms to go off before detecting an attack, you're already too late. The best hackers today don't trigger alarms—they blend in, manipulate data, and slowly sabotage industrial systems.

With AI-powered anomaly detection, behavioral analytics, and threat intelligence, you can spot cyber threats before they cause real damage.

Key Takeaways:

✓ Anomalies = The first sign of cyberattacks.

✓ Hackers hide by mimicking normal behavior—don't let them.

✓ AI & behavioral analytics can catch subtle cyber threats.

✓ Correlating data sources gives deeper visibility.

✓ Threat intelligence helps detect attacks before they start.

Bottom line? If you want to catch cyberattacks before they wreck your factory, start monitoring for the weird, the unusual, and the unexpected. Because when it comes to industrial cybersecurity, if something feels off, it probably is. 🚨

9.3 Incident Response Strategies for Industrial Environments

When Everything Hits the Fan: Cyber Incidents in Industrial Networks

Let's be real—no matter how many firewalls, intrusion detection systems, and security best practices you throw at your industrial network, at some point, something is going to go horribly wrong.

Maybe it's ransomware locking down your SCADA system, or a mysterious PLC suddenly running rogue commands at 2 AM. Or worse—your production line grinds to a halt, and someone yells, "Why is the robotic arm making TikTok dance moves instead of assembling parts?!"

When the cyber chaos unfolds, you don't want to be the person Googling "how to handle an ICS security breach" in real-time. That's why having a solid incident response (IR) strategy is non-negotiable in industrial environments.

So, grab a coffee (or something stronger), and let's break down how to detect, contain, and recover from an industrial cyber incident before your factory turns into a crime scene.

Why Incident Response in ICS/SCADA is Different from IT

Incident response in IT is all about protecting data and networks. But in industrial environments, the stakes are way higher:

IT Incident: "Oh no, our email server is down. We'll fix it soon."

OT Incident: "Oh no, the cooling system is offline. The plant might explode."

A cyberattack on an OT (Operational Technology) system doesn't just result in stolen data—it can cause physical destruction, production downtime, and even safety hazards. That's why industrial environments need a customized, high-stakes incident response plan that considers both cybersecurity and physical process safety.

The 6 Phases of Incident Response in Industrial Networks

A well-planned ICS incident response strategy follows a structured approach. Here's how to handle an attack like a pro:

1. Preparation: Expect the Worst, Train Like a Madman

The worst time to plan for an incident is during the incident. Preparation is everything.

✅ Create an ICS-Specific Incident Response Plan (IRP)

Who does what when an attack happens? Define roles clearly.

Identify critical assets (PLCs, SCADA, sensors) and their dependencies.

Ensure compliance with NIST CSF, IEC 62443, and NERC CIP standards.

✅ Train the Incident Response Team (IRT)

Conduct tabletop exercises and red team/blue team drills.

Simulate ICS-specific attack scenarios (e.g., ransomware in SCADA, MITM on Modbus).

✅ Pre-Deploy Forensic and Monitoring Tools

Set up logs, intrusion detection systems (IDS), and network segmentation before an attack happens.

Use ICS-specific security tools like Dragos, Nozomi Networks, and Claroty.

🔊 **Example**: A power plant simulated a ransomware attack on their control room systems. The drill exposed a 20-minute delay in response time—so they improved their escalation process and reduced it to 5 minutes.

2. Detection & Analysis: Finding the Needle in a Haystack

Most ICS cyberattacks don't announce themselves—they lurk in the shadows, manipulating industrial processes quietly.

✅ Use AI-Powered Anomaly Detection

Monitor for unexpected changes in PLC commands, sensor data, and network traffic.

Deploy real-time threat intelligence feeds for early warning.

✅ Correlate Security Alerts Across IT and OT

Just because IT isn't showing signs of compromise doesn't mean OT is safe.

Check firewall logs, SCADA alerts, and physical sensor readings together.

✅ Contain the Blast Radius

Segment infected systems from critical operations.

Use industrial firewalls and one-way data diodes to isolate threats.

🔊 **Example**: A hacker compromised a smart water treatment facility, slowly adjusting chemical levels. Anomaly detection tools caught irregular PLC behavior and stopped the attack before contaminated water reached the public.

3. Containment: Stop the Bleeding

Once a cyberattack is confirmed, contain it fast before it spreads.

✅ Short-Term Containment

Disconnect infected devices (if safe to do so).

Disable remote access for ICS components.

Freeze automated control actions to prevent further damage.

✅ **Long-Term Containment**

Patch vulnerabilities to prevent re-entry by attackers.

Implement new firewall rules and access controls.

Review and validate backups before restoring.

📖 **Example**: A factory dealing with ICS ransomware had network segmentation in place. They quickly isolated infected SCADA terminals, preventing malware from reaching the PLCs controlling production.

4. Eradication: Get Rid of the Cyber Cockroaches

Once the attack is contained, it's time to clean up the mess.

✅ **Remove Malware and Persistent Threats**

Scan for backdoors, trojans, and rogue scripts.

Verify that PLCs and HMIs have not been reprogrammed by attackers.

✅ **Patch & Harden Systems**

Update vulnerable software, firmware, and network configurations.

Implement multi-factor authentication (MFA) for remote access.

📖 **Example**: A manufacturing plant removed a stealthy backdoor in their SCADA servers, which had been sitting undetected for 6 months, waiting to launch an attack.

5. Recovery: Bring Systems Back Online—Safely

Now it's time to restore normal operations, but don't rush it.

✅ **Test Restored Systems in a Sandbox**

Ensure that PLC logic and SCADA configurations are intact.

Run simulation tests before reconnecting live systems.

✅ **Monitor for Residual Threats**

Some attacks leave hidden time bombs—monitor closely for anomalies.

🔍 **Example**: A logistics company restored their warehouse automation systems after a cyberattack, only to find that a malware variant had remained hidden in a backup. Always verify backups before deploying.

6. Lessons Learned: Make Sure It Never Happens Again

After an incident, document everything and improve defenses.

✅ **Conduct a Post-Incident Review**

What went wrong? What worked well?

Update incident response plans based on findings.

✅ **Share Intelligence with Industry Peers**

Report new attack tactics to ICS-CERT, ISACs, and cybersecurity forums.

🔍 **Example**: After being hit by a sophisticated ransomware attack, a steel manufacturer rewrote its security policies, improved employee training, and deployed better network segmentation. They never got hit again.

Final Thoughts: Be Ready, Not Reactive

If you wait until an attack happens to think about incident response, you've already lost. In industrial environments, speed, preparation, and automation are the difference between a minor disruption and a full-blown catastrophe.

Key Takeaways:

✓□ **Prepare BEFORE an attack**—train your team & set up defenses.

✓□ Detect threats early using AI, anomaly detection, and behavioral analysis.

✓□ Contain the threat FAST before it spreads to critical systems.

✓□ Eradicate malware, patch vulnerabilities, and verify backups.

✓□ Recover operations SAFELY—test everything before going live.

✓□ Learn from incidents to prevent future attacks.

Cyberattacks on industrial systems are inevitable—but disaster isn't. If you're proactive, prepared, and paranoid, you can handle any cyber threat like a boss.

Now go update your incident response plan—your factory's future depends on it. 🚀

9.4 Using AI and Machine Learning for IIoT Threat Detection

AI to the Rescue: When Hackers Get Smarter, So Should We

Let's face it—hackers aren't taking coffee breaks anymore. They're leveraging automation, AI, and advanced exploits to break into Industrial IoT (IIoT) systems faster than ever. And if we're still relying on outdated rule-based security systems, we might as well be defending our smart factories with duct tape and optimism.

This is where Artificial Intelligence (AI) and Machine Learning (ML) step in as our cyber bodyguards. Think of them as Iron Man's suit for cybersecurity—constantly evolving, detecting patterns, and shutting down threats before they can cause havoc. No more relying on slow, manual threat hunting—AI is here to fight cybercrime at machine speed.

But before we start celebrating our AI overlords, let's break down how these futuristic technologies are revolutionizing IIoT threat detection, making industrial security smarter, faster, and way more effective.

Why Traditional Threat Detection Fails in IIoT

Legacy cybersecurity methods—like signature-based antivirus software, static firewall rules, and manual threat hunting—are about as useful against modern cyber threats as a wooden shield in a gunfight.

Here's why traditional defenses struggle in industrial environments:

IIoT Generates Massive Data Volumes

A smart factory produces terabytes of sensor data, logs, and machine communications. Humans can't manually analyze this tsunami of information fast enough.

Attacks Are Becoming More Sophisticated

Hackers use AI-powered malware, zero-day exploits, and living-off-the-land techniques to bypass traditional security measures.

Industrial Networks Are Highly Dynamic

ICS/SCADA networks aren't static—they evolve with new devices, firmware updates, and reconfigurations. Static security rules can't keep up.

Signature-Based Detection is Too Slow

By the time a new threat signature is added to a database, the attack has already caused damage.

The solution? AI-powered threat detection that adapts in real-time.

How AI and ML Improve IIoT Threat Detection

AI and ML don't just replace traditional security—they supercharge it. Here's how they make IIoT cybersecurity smarter and more proactive:

1. Anomaly Detection: Catching Cyber Threats Before They Strike

🔍 **How It Works**: AI continuously monitors network traffic, device behavior, and operational processes. Instead of looking for known attack signatures, it learns what "normal" looks like—and flags anything unusual.

🚨 **Example:**

A PLC that normally sends temperature data every 5 minutes suddenly starts sending thousands of commands per second.

AI flags this as an anomaly, potentially preventing a ransomware attack or a cyber-physical sabotage.

Why It's Powerful:

✓☐ Detects zero-day attacks and unknown threats.
✓☐ Doesn't rely on outdated blacklists or pre-defined signatures.
✓☐ Adapts in real-time to new attack patterns.

2. Behavioral Analysis: Spotting Malicious Activity from Insiders and Attackers

🔍 **How It Works**: Instead of just monitoring devices, AI tracks user behavior—who logs in, what they access, and how they interact with industrial systems.

🎥 **Example:**

A maintenance worker suddenly accesses PLC configurations at 2 AM from an unauthorized remote IP address.

AI immediately flags this as a potential insider threat or compromised credentials.

Why It's Powerful:

✓☐ Detects internal threats and compromised accounts.
✓☐ Stops attackers who use stolen credentials to blend in.
✓☐ Monitors for suspicious access patterns in real-time.

3. Predictive Threat Intelligence: Forecasting Future Attacks

🔍 **How It Works**: AI analyzes historical cyber incidents, attack patterns, and security logs to predict the most likely threats before they occur.

🎥 **Example:**

If a specific ransomware strain is attacking smart factories globally, AI warns your security team in advance—giving them time to patch vulnerabilities before the attack reaches your network.

Why It's Powerful:

✓☐ Provides early warnings based on global threat intelligence.
✓☐ Helps organizations proactively patch vulnerabilities before they're exploited.
✓☐ Reduces reaction time, making cyber defenses more efficient.

4. Automated Incident Response: Fighting Back in Real Time

🔍 **How It Works**: AI-powered security systems don't just detect threats—they respond automatically, blocking attacks before they spread.

📸 **Example:**

A hacker tries to launch a man-in-the-middle (MITM) attack on a Modbus network.

AI detects the unauthorized packet injection, isolates the affected device, and blocks malicious traffic instantly—all without human intervention.

Why It's Powerful:

✓☐ Stops attacks in milliseconds, preventing major damage.
✓☐ Reduces human error in threat response.
✓☐ Scales infinitely across large industrial networks.

Challenges of AI in Industrial Cybersecurity

AI is a game-changer, but it's not perfect. Here are some challenges to consider:

☐ **False Positives:**

AI sometimes flags normal behavior as suspicious, leading to alert fatigue for security teams.

☐ **Adversarial AI Attacks:**

Hackers can manipulate AI models by feeding them misleading data.

☐ **Implementation Complexity:**

Integrating AI with legacy ICS/SCADA systems can be difficult.

The solution? Human-AI collaboration. AI should augment human security teams, not replace them.

Real-World Case Study: AI Saves a Power Plant from Cyber Attack

🔎 **Scenario:**

A hydroelectric power plant in Europe started experiencing unexpected fluctuations in turbine control systems. Engineers initially dismissed it as a software glitch.

🔎 **What AI Found:**

AI-powered security tools detected a slow-moving cyberattack, where hackers were gradually increasing turbine speeds to cause mechanical failure.

🔎 **The Outcome:**

AI flagged the abnormal behavior before physical damage occurred.

Security teams isolated the compromised PLCs and blocked attacker access.

A potential disaster was prevented—saving millions in damages.

Final Thoughts: AI is the Future of Industrial Cybersecurity

AI and machine learning are not just buzzwords—they are essential for protecting industrial environments from modern cyber threats.

Key Takeaways:

✓□ AI-powered anomaly detection finds cyber threats before they strike.
✓□ Behavioral analysis detects insider threats and stolen credentials.
✓□ Predictive threat intelligence gives early warnings of attacks.
✓□ Automated incident response stops attacks in real-time.
✓□ AI works best when combined with human expertise—not as a replacement.

As cyber threats evolve, so must our defenses. If hackers are using AI to break into IIoT systems, it's time we use AI to stop them.

So, will AI save your smart factory from the next cyberattack? Maybe. But only if you deploy it before the hackers do. 🚀

9.5 Building a Cyber Resilient Industrial Infrastructure

Cyber Resilience: Because Hackers Don't Take Sick Days

Let's be honest—no cybersecurity system is 100% bulletproof. If anyone tells you otherwise, they're probably trying to sell you something (or they've been living under a rock since the 90s). The reality is that industrial environments will get hacked—the real question is, how well can they recover?

That's where cyber resilience comes in. It's not just about preventing attacks—it's about surviving them and bouncing back stronger. Think of it like a boxing match: you're going to take some punches, but if you can stay on your feet and keep swinging, you're still in the fight.

So, how do we make Industrial IoT (IIoT) and SCADA systems tough enough to handle whatever cybercriminals throw at them? Buckle up, because we're about to break down the key strategies for building a cyber-resilient industrial infrastructure.

What is Cyber Resilience, and Why Does It Matter?

Cyber resilience is not just cybersecurity—it's a holistic approach to surviving cyber threats. It includes:

✅ **Prevention**: Stopping attacks before they happen.
✅ **Detection**: Identifying threats as soon as they occur.
✅ **Response**: Reacting quickly and effectively to minimize damage.
✅ **Recovery**: Getting back to normal without major downtime.

For industrial environments, resilience is critical because:

⚡ **Downtime = Massive Financial Losses**

A single hour of downtime in a smart factory or power plant can cost millions.

⚡ Physical Safety is on the Line

A cyber attack on SCADA systems controlling water treatment, oil refineries, or power grids isn't just about stolen data—it can physically harm people.

⚡ Hackers are Playing the Long Game

Some cyberattacks aren't instant—they stay hidden for months, waiting for the perfect moment to strike.

So, how do we prepare for the worst while hoping for the best?

1. Implementing a Strong Industrial Defense Strategy

Just like a medieval castle had multiple layers of defense (moats, walls, guards, and maybe a dragon or two ☐), industrial environments need multi-layered security.

◆ Network Segmentation

Keep IT and OT networks separate so hackers can't jump from a hacked corporate email to a critical SCADA system.

◆ Zero Trust Security Model

Assume that no device or user can be trusted by default—always verify before granting access.

◆ Strong Authentication & Access Control

Ditch default passwords (seriously, "admin/admin" should be illegal).

Implement multi-factor authentication (MFA) for critical systems.

◆ Endpoint Protection for IIoT Devices

Many IIoT devices lack built-in security—deploy AI-driven endpoint security tools to monitor them in real-time.

2. Real-Time Threat Detection & AI-Driven Monitoring

If you're still relying on manual log reviews to catch cyber threats, you might as well be using a sundial to check the time. AI-powered monitoring and threat detection are a must.

🔍 Behavioral Anomaly Detection

AI learns what "normal" traffic and device behavior look like—then flags anything suspicious.

⚡ Predictive Threat Intelligence

Uses machine learning to predict attacks before they happen, based on global cyber trends.

🔘 Automated Response Systems

If an ICS device starts behaving oddly, an AI-driven system can isolate it instantly—stopping an attack before it spreads.

3. Incident Response Planning: Because Panic is Not a Strategy

When a cyberattack happens, the worst thing you can do is panic. (Okay, maybe the worst thing is paying ransomware attackers immediately—but panic is a close second.)

Every industrial organization needs a tested incident response plan that includes:

📜 Clear Roles & Responsibilities

Everyone should know their role during a cyber event—from the security team to the factory floor operators.

🚀 Rapid Containment & Isolation Protocols

If an attack happens, affected systems should be quarantined immediately to prevent spread.

☐☐ Backup & Recovery Playbooks

Test backups regularly—because "we have backups" is useless if they don't actually work.

🔊 Crisis Communication Plans

Cyber incidents can be PR nightmares. Be ready with a plan for internal and external communication.

4. Backup, Redundancy & Disaster Recovery: The Cybersecurity Safety Net

If you're relying on a single, untested backup, you might as well not have one. Cyber resilience means having multiple recovery options.

💾 Regular Data Backups (And Testing!)

Keep offline, air-gapped backups safe from ransomware.

Test backups frequently to ensure they're actually recoverable.

☐ Redundant Critical Systems

If one system fails, another should take over instantly—this is especially critical for SCADA environments controlling power grids or water systems.

☐☐ Failover & Hot Standby Systems

Automatic failover mechanisms ensure that critical operations continue even if an attack takes down primary systems.

5. Continuous Security Training & Awareness: Humans are the Weakest (and Strongest) Link

No matter how strong your cybersecurity tech is, a well-placed phishing email can still take it all down.

👥 Security Awareness Training for OT & IT Teams

Train employees to recognize social engineering tactics, phishing attempts, and insider threats.

🔴🔵 Red Team vs. Blue Team Drills

Run cyberattack simulations to test how well your team detects and responds to threats.

🔄 Continuous Improvement & Security Culture

Cyber resilience isn't a one-time thing—it's an ongoing process of learning and adapting.

Final Thoughts: Cyber Resilience is a Mindset, Not Just a Tech Stack

Cybersecurity is like physical fitness—you don't just go to the gym once and call it a day. It's an ongoing process of strengthening, adapting, and preparing.

Key Takeaways:

✓ Cyber resilience = cybersecurity + recovery + adaptability.
✓ Layered defense strategies (segmentation, Zero Trust, AI monitoring) are a must.
✓ Incident response planning prevents chaos during a breach.
✓ Backups and redundancy ensure quick recovery.
✓ Security training keeps employees from being the weakest link.

The goal isn't to prevent every single attack—that's impossible. The goal is to build an industrial infrastructure that can take the hit, keep running, and fight back.

Because let's be real—hackers aren't going away anytime soon. So let's make their job as miserable as possible. 🚀

Chapter 10: Future Trends and Best Practices in IIoT Security

Let's be real—cyber threats evolve faster than your boss can approve a security budget. Today's cutting-edge defenses might be tomorrow's obsolete tech, especially with advancements in AI, quantum computing, and blockchain. The future of IIoT security is a constant game of cat and mouse, where hackers innovate just as fast as defenders do. So, what's next? Are we headed for a world where machines defend themselves? Will AI-powered IIoT security make hackers irrelevant? Or are we just one bad firmware update away from Skynet?

This chapter looks at the future of IIoT security, covering emerging technologies such as AI-driven threat detection, blockchain for device authentication, and quantum-resistant cryptography. We'll also discuss secure-by-design principles for next-generation IIoT deployments, risk management frameworks, and the evolving threat landscape. Finally, we'll explore red team vs. blue team strategies and compliance best practices to help organizations stay ahead of cyber threats.

10.1 The Role of AI, Blockchain, and Quantum Computing in IIoT Security

Welcome to the Future: Where Hackers Get Hacked Back

Let's get something straight: the cyber battlefield is evolving faster than ever. Yesterday's firewalls and antivirus software are about as useful as a medieval knight bringing a sword to a drone fight. If you're still relying on traditional security methods, you're already losing.

But don't worry—technology is on our side too. In the arms race between attackers and defenders, we now have some seriously game-changing weapons: Artificial Intelligence (AI), Blockchain, and Quantum Computing.

Imagine AI acting like an ultra-fast security guard, blockchain as an unhackable logbook, and quantum computing as a math wizard that can crack (or reinforce) any encryption in the blink of an eye. Sounds like sci-fi? Well, this is the new reality of IIoT security. Let's break it all down.

AI in IIoT Security: The Cyber Bodyguard That Never Sleeps

Hackers don't work 9-to-5 jobs. They attack at 2 AM on a holiday weekend when no one is watching. That's why AI-driven cybersecurity is a game-changer—it never takes a break.

How AI is Reinventing Industrial Security

☐ Threat Detection at Superhuman Speed

AI analyzes millions of data points in real-time, spotting anomalies that a human would miss.

If a hacker tries to inject malicious code into a SCADA system, AI can detect and shut it down before it spreads.

● Automated Incident Response

AI-powered Security Information and Event Management (SIEM) systems can automatically isolate compromised devices to prevent network-wide infection.

Imagine your factory's IIoT sensors suddenly sending weird signals—AI can quarantine them before they cause a catastrophic failure.

☉ Predicting Attacks Before They Happen

Machine learning models analyze past attacks to predict and prevent future breaches.

AI hunts down vulnerabilities in your network before hackers find them.

👀 Deep Packet Inspection & Behavioral Analysis

AI can inspect every single packet of network traffic, identifying malware and unauthorized access attempts.

If an employee logs in from an unusual location, AI can trigger an alert or even block access.

But let's be real—AI isn't perfect. If hackers can trick AI models (poisoning data or mimicking normal behavior), they can slip through unnoticed. That's where blockchain comes in.

Blockchain: Turning Cybersecurity Into a Digital Fort Knox

Blockchain isn't just for Bitcoin millionaires—it's actually a powerful security tool for IIoT environments. Here's why:

Why Blockchain is a Big Deal for IIoT Security

📜 Tamper-Proof Data Logs

Once data is recorded on a blockchain, it can't be altered or deleted—which makes it perfect for audit trails and forensic investigations.

If a hacker tries to cover their tracks, blockchain ensures that all logs remain untouched and verifiable.

🔗 Decentralized Security

Traditional security models rely on a central authority (which can be hacked).

Blockchain eliminates single points of failure, making attacks significantly harder.

✅ Secure Device Authentication

Each IIoT device can be assigned a unique blockchain-based identity, preventing hackers from spoofing or impersonating devices.

This is crucial for SCADA and ICS environments, where unauthorized device access can cause catastrophic failures.

💳 Smart Contracts for Automated Security

Smart contracts can automatically enforce security policies—for example, blocking devices that don't meet compliance standards.

If a PLC in a factory isn't running the latest firmware, it could be automatically isolated from the network.

Of course, blockchain has limitations—it can be slow, requires high computational power, and isn't ideal for real-time threat detection. That's where quantum computing enters the chat.

Quantum Computing: The Ultimate Cybersecurity Double-Edged Sword

Quantum computing is like giving a hacker a rocket launcher—but also giving cyber defenders a force field. It's both a huge threat and a revolutionary security tool.

The Good: How Quantum Computing Enhances IIoT Security

🔐 Quantum Encryption (Quantum Key Distribution - QKD)

Quantum encryption is theoretically unbreakable—if a hacker tries to eavesdrop, the system knows instantly.

This makes it impossible to intercept IIoT communications without detection.

⚡ Supercharged Threat Analysis

Quantum computers can process cybersecurity data at speeds unimaginable with classical computers.

A quantum AI system could analyze industrial network traffic in real-time, instantly detecting sophisticated threats.

🚀 Post-Quantum Cryptography

Researchers are developing new encryption methods that even quantum computers can't break—making IIoT systems future-proof against quantum attacks.

The Bad: The Quantum Threat to Cybersecurity

💣 Breaking Traditional Encryption in Seconds

RSA, ECC, and most current encryption methods would be obsolete the moment quantum computers become powerful enough.

Hackers (or governments) with access to quantum computers could decrypt sensitive industrial data effortlessly.

☐☐ Nation-State Quantum Espionage

Countries like China, the US, and Russia are racing to develop quantum computing for intelligence and cybersecurity warfare.

Any organization not preparing for the quantum shift is already behind.

Final Thoughts: The Future of IIoT Security is Here—Are You Ready?

IIoT security isn't about playing defense anymore—it's about building resilient, self-defending systems that fight back.

Key Takeaways:

✓☐ AI makes cybersecurity proactive, detecting threats before they cause damage.
✓☐ Blockchain ensures tamper-proof logs and decentralized security.
✓☐ Quantum computing is a double-edged sword—it can either revolutionize security or break everything we rely on.
✓☐ The best IIoT security strategy? Combine AI, blockchain, and quantum-resistant cryptography.

In short, the hackers of tomorrow will have AI, blockchain exploits, and quantum attacks at their disposal. But if we adopt these technologies first, we can stay ahead of the curve and keep our smart factories, grids, and industrial environments secure.

Because let's face it—we don't want the future of IIoT security to look like a dystopian cyberpunk nightmare. 🚀

10.2 Secure IIoT Design Principles for Next-Generation Smart Factories

Welcome to the Smart Factory—Now Let's Keep It from Getting Hacked

Alright, let's get something straight—smart factories are awesome. They've got robots building robots, AI optimizing production lines, and sensors monitoring everything from temperature to vibration levels. But you know what they also have? Hackers trying to turn all that automation into a giant ransomware jackpot.

Imagine your entire factory grinding to a halt because some script kiddie in their basement figured out how to exploit a weak IIoT device. Or worse, a nation-state actor hijacking your industrial control systems. Sounds like a sci-fi horror movie, right? Well, it's already happening.

That's why we're here. Designing security into IIoT from the ground up isn't just a good idea—it's an absolute necessity. Let's talk about how to build the next generation of smart factories without making them an all-you-can-hack buffet for cybercriminals.

Principle #1: Security by Design (Not as an Afterthought!)

If you build a house, you don't add the locks after someone breaks in, right? The same goes for IIoT security.

Many industrial environments deploy smart devices first, then panic about security later. This is how you end up with unpatched PLCs from the early 2000s still running critical operations. Instead, security must be baked into the architecture from day one.

How to Implement Security by Design

◆ **Use Secure Hardware** – Select IIoT devices that have built-in security features, such as hardware-based encryption, secure boot, and tamper detection.

◆ **Zero-Trust Architecture** – Assume that everything is a potential security risk—every sensor, actuator, and industrial controller should be authenticated and monitored.

◆ **Default to Secure Settings** – Many IIoT devices ship with default credentials like "admin/admin" (which hackers LOVE). Require strong passwords and enforce security policies at deployment.

◆ **Regular Security Audits** – Just because your IIoT network was secure last year doesn't mean it's secure today. Continuous testing and updating are essential.

Principle #2: Network Segmentation & Least Privilege Access

Would you give every employee in a factory access to the CEO's bank account? No? Then why do so many IIoT environments allow every device to talk to everything else on the network?

Hackers love flat networks because once they get in, they can move laterally and take down entire production lines.

How to Stop Hackers from Moving Around Your Network

◆ **Segment IT and OT Networks** – Keep corporate networks (IT) separate from industrial control networks (OT) with firewalls and strict access controls.

◆ **Micro-Segmentation** – Break industrial networks into smaller, isolated zones so that if one device is compromised, it can't take everything else down.

◆ **Role-Based Access Control (RBAC)** – Not every engineer, technician, or system should have full admin access. Least privilege access should be the rule.

◆ **Network Monitoring & Anomaly Detection** – Use AI-powered network security tools to identify suspicious behavior in real time.

Principle #3: Secure Communication Protocols (Because Plaintext is for Amateurs)

If your IIoT devices are sending data over the network without encryption, you might as well be shouting your passwords in a crowded room.

Industrial protocols like Modbus, DNP3, and MQTT weren't designed with security in mind—but that doesn't mean we can't make them safer.

How to Secure IIoT Communications

◆ **Use TLS/SSL for Data Encryption** – Any data traveling between IIoT devices should be encrypted to prevent eavesdropping and tampering.

◆ **Implement Secure Versions of Protocols** – Use Secure OPC-UA instead of plain OPC-UA, and always disable legacy insecure options.

◆ **Validate and Authenticate Devices** – Deploy certificate-based authentication to ensure that only trusted devices can communicate.

◆ **Monitor for Protocol Exploits** – Hackers use MITM (Man-in-the-Middle) attacks and replay attacks to manipulate IIoT traffic. Use deep packet inspection tools to detect and stop them.

Principle #4: Continuous Patch Management (No More "Set It and Forget It")

If your IIoT devices are still running firmware from five years ago, congratulations—you're a hacker's dream target.

A shocking number of ICS/SCADA devices never get updated because operators are afraid of breaking something. But leaving unpatched vulnerabilities exposes your entire smart factory to cyberattacks.

How to Keep IIoT Firmware Secure

✦ **Automate Patch Management** – Deploy automated tools to keep IIoT firmware up to date without disrupting production.

✦ **Implement Redundancy Before Updating** – Use failover systems so that if an update causes an issue, you can roll back safely.

✦ **Don't Trust Vendors Blindly** – Validate and test firmware updates before deployment—because sometimes patches introduce new vulnerabilities.

Principle #5: AI-Powered Threat Detection & Incident Response

Let's be real—human security teams can't manually monitor thousands of IIoT devices. That's why AI-driven security solutions are the future.

Instead of waiting for a breach, AI can detect and stop threats before they cause damage.

How AI Enhances IIoT Security

☐ **Anomaly Detection** – AI learns what "normal behavior" looks like and flags unusual activity (like a compromised sensor sending rogue commands).

☐ **Automated Threat Response** – AI can isolate infected devices, block malicious traffic, and alert security teams instantly.

🔍 **Predictive Security** – Machine learning models analyze past attacks to predict and prevent new threats.

Final Thoughts: The Future of IIoT Security is Proactive, Not Reactive

Securing next-gen smart factories isn't about just throwing firewalls at the problem—it's about building cybersecurity into every layer of the infrastructure.

Key Takeaways:

✓☐ **Security by Design** – Secure IIoT from the ground up, not as an afterthought.

✓☐ **Network Segmentation** – Don't let hackers move freely inside your industrial environment.

✓☐ **Encrypted Communications** – No more plaintext protocols! Secure every data exchange.

✓☐ **Patch, Patch, Patch** – Regular firmware updates are non-negotiable.

✓☐ **AI-Driven Security** – Let AI detect, prevent, and respond to cyber threats before they escalate.

At the end of the day, you don't want your smart factory to turn into a cybercriminal's playground. The future of IIoT depends on proactive security, not crisis control.

And remember—the best way to stop a cyberattack is to make sure it never happens in the first place. 🔒🛡️

10.3 Red Team vs. Blue Team Strategies for Industrial Security

Welcome to the Cybersecurity Battle Arena

Imagine this: your factory is a high-tech fortress, filled with robotic arms, industrial controllers, and sensors talking to each other like an AI-powered symphony. Everything's running smoothly… until someone unplugs a critical PLC, injects malicious Modbus commands, and suddenly—your perfectly tuned assembly line is producing nothing but chaos.

Who did it? Was it a cybercriminal? A disgruntled insider? A nation-state actor? Or—plot twist—was it one of your own security professionals?

Welcome to the world of Red Team vs. Blue Team cybersecurity. One side attacks. The other defends. And in the brutal landscape of Industrial IoT (IIoT), both teams are equally crucial to keeping your smart factory from turning into a hacked, ransomware-ridden mess.

What is Red Teaming? (The Hackers in Your Own House)

The Red Team is your in-house group of ethical hackers who think like real-world attackers. Their job? Break into your systems before the bad guys do.

● They simulate cyberattacks on your factory, finding vulnerabilities before someone exploits them.
● They use real hacking tools, techniques, and procedures (TTPs) to test your defenses.
● They play the role of cybercriminals, insiders, and even advanced persistent threats (APTs).

Red Team Techniques in Industrial Security

💀 **Phishing and Social Engineering** – Can your employees spot a fake login page or a malicious USB stick labeled "Q3 Salary Data"? (Spoiler: probably not.)

💀 **Network Penetration Testing** – They try to breach your IIoT and OT networks using real-world attack vectors like MITM attacks, protocol exploitation, and weak credentials.

💀 **SCADA & ICS Exploits** – Red Teamers will hunt for unpatched SCADA vulnerabilities, misconfigured PLCs, and exposed industrial protocols like Modbus or DNP3.

💀 **Physical Security Testing** – Can they walk into your plant, plug into a network port, and hijack control systems? You'd be surprised how often a clipboard and a confident attitude can bypass security.

The Red Team's goal isn't to "win"—it's to expose weaknesses so the Blue Team can strengthen the defenses.

What is Blue Teaming? (The Digital Guardians of the Factory Floor)

If the Red Team is the chaos crew, the Blue Team is the last line of defense. These are the cybersecurity defenders, the digital firefighters, the ones who get the call when something goes horribly wrong.

● They monitor the network, hunt for threats, and respond to incidents.

● They build layers of defense to make the Red Team's job harder.

● They use threat intelligence, log analysis, and AI-driven security to detect breaches before they spread.

Blue Team Strategies for Protecting IIoT Environments

☐ **Network Segmentation & Zero Trust** – Keeping IT and OT separate, enforcing strict access controls, and not trusting any device by default.

☐ **Real-Time Monitoring & Anomaly Detection** – Using SIEM (Security Information and Event Management) tools to spot malicious behavior in industrial networks.

☐ **Incident Response Drills** – Practicing "what if" scenarios, so when a ransomware attack hits, nobody panics, and the response is swift.

☐ **Patch & Vulnerability Management** – Regularly updating firmware, closing security gaps, and removing default passwords from IIoT devices.

The Ultimate Battle: How Red & Blue Teams Work Together

The real power of Red and Blue teaming isn't in competition—it's in collaboration. That's why many organizations adopt a "Purple Team" approach, where both sides work together to improve security.

☐ Red Team hacks. Blue Team detects. They compare notes, improve defenses, and repeat the process until breaking in becomes nearly impossible.

☐ Blue Team learns attack techniques. The Red Team teaches defenders how real-world threats operate, so they can develop stronger security measures.

☐ Red Team sharpens their skills. The harder it gets to break in, the more advanced the attacks become, making the whole security posture stronger.

Final Thoughts: Your Smart Factory Needs Both Attackers and Defenders

Cybersecurity isn't a one-and-done deal. Hackers evolve. Threats change. And if you're not constantly testing your security, you're already behind.

Key Takeaways:

✓☐ Red Teaming is about finding and exploiting vulnerabilities before real hackers do.

✓☐ Blue Teaming is about defending, detecting, and responding to threats in real time.

✓☐ The best security strategy is a mix of both—attack to test, defend to improve.

✓☐ If you're not running Red vs. Blue Team exercises, you're leaving your IIoT environment wide open.

At the end of the day, the best way to secure your factory is to keep breaking it—before someone else does. 🚀 🔒

10.4 Compliance and Risk Management in IIoT Security Programs

Why Compliance Feels Like Homework (But You Can't Ignore It)

Let's be real—nobody wakes up excited about compliance. It's like getting a root canal: you don't want it, but skipping it leads to much bigger pain later. In Industrial IoT (IIoT), compliance isn't just about following rules—it's about not getting hacked, fined, or shut down because your security was as strong as a wet paper bag.

Regulations like NIST, IEC 62443, NERC CIP, and GDPR weren't created just to make your life miserable. They exist because hackers love weak industrial security, and governments don't want their power grids, water treatment plants, or factories turned into cyber chaos zones. Skipping compliance isn't just risky—it's an open invitation for attackers.

But don't worry—I've got you. Let's break down compliance and risk management into something that won't put you to sleep.

What is Compliance in IIoT Security? (And Why You Should Care)

Compliance is a set of rules, standards, and best practices that ensure your IIoT environment is secure before something bad happens. It's basically the cybersecurity playbook that auditors, regulators, and insurance companies expect you to follow.

Key Compliance Frameworks in IIoT Security

☐ **NIST Cybersecurity Framework** – The "golden rule" of cybersecurity. It helps organizations identify, protect, detect, respond, and recover from cyber threats.

☐ **IEC 62443** – The bible of industrial cybersecurity, designed specifically for ICS, SCADA, and IIoT environments. If you're in manufacturing, energy, or any critical infrastructure, you NEED this.

☐ **NERC CIP (North American Electric Reliability Corporation** – Critical Infrastructure Protection) – If your factory controls energy grids or power plants, you better believe regulators will fine you into oblivion if you ignore this.

☐ **ISO 27001** – The global standard for information security management systems (ISMS), covering data protection, risk management, and business continuity.

☐ **GDPR & CCPA** – If your IIoT devices handle personal data (think smart meters, medical IoT, or connected cars), violating privacy laws can cost you millions in fines.

Long story short: compliance isn't optional. It's the price of admission if you want to stay in business without making headlines for a catastrophic data breach.

Risk Management: Identifying & Reducing Cyber Risks

While compliance gives you the rulebook, risk management is about applying those rules in a way that actually works for your specific IIoT setup.

How to Build a Risk Management Program for IIoT

🔊 **Step 1: Identify Critical Assets** – Make a list of all connected devices, industrial controllers, and networked systems that, if hacked, could cause major damage.

🔊 **Step 2: Assess Risks** – Look at where your vulnerabilities are, from outdated SCADA systems to weak authentication on IIoT devices.

🔊 **Step 3: Implement Controls** – Use firewalls, network segmentation, encryption, multi-factor authentication (MFA), and security monitoring to mitigate risks.

🔊 **Step 4: Monitor and Improve** – Cyber threats evolve daily. A good risk management program constantly adapts to new threats.

Think of risk management as cybersecurity chess: The goal isn't just to defend—it's to stay three steps ahead of the hackers.

Compliance Without Pain: Making It Work for Your Factory

● **Myth**: Compliance is just paperwork.

✓ **Reality**: It's about reducing real-world risks that could cripple your industrial operations.

● **Myth**: Compliance kills innovation.

✓ **Reality**: It forces you to implement security best practices—which actually makes your IIoT systems more resilient and scalable.

● **Myth**: We're too small to be targeted.

✓ **Reality**: Hackers LOVE small factories because they usually have the weakest security. Even ransomware gangs target mom-and-pop manufacturing plants.

Final Thoughts: Compliance & Risk Management Aren't Optional

If you think compliance is expensive, try getting hacked. Cybercriminals don't care how big or small your factory is—if they can breach your IIoT systems, they will.

Here's what you should take away:

✓ Compliance protects your business from cyber threats, legal fines, and operational disasters.
✓ Risk management helps you understand where you're vulnerable—so you can fix it before attackers exploit it.
✓ Ignoring security in IIoT isn't just risky—it's a guaranteed way to become a hacker's next target.

So, do your future self a favor: treat compliance and risk management like cybersecurity armor. Without it, you're just waiting to be breached. 🔒🚀

10.5 Emerging Threats and Future Challenges in ICS/SCADA Security

Welcome to the Future—Where Cyber Threats Are Even More Terrifying

Remember when industrial security was just about keeping the machines running and hoping no one accidentally unplugged something important? Well, those were the good old days. Now, your factory floor is a battlefield, and cybercriminals aren't just script kiddies trying to deface your website. They're nation-states, ransomware cartels, and black-hat hackers looking to shut you down, steal trade secrets, or even cause physical destruction.

And guess what? The threats are only getting worse. As we step into the future of smart factories, hyper-connected ICS, AI-driven automation, and edge computing, attackers are evolving faster than most companies can adapt. So, let's talk about what's coming next, what you should be worried about, and how to stay ahead of the game.

The Next Wave of ICS/SCADA Security Threats

If you thought ransomware was bad, buckle up—because the next generation of cyber threats is even scarier. Here are some of the biggest security nightmares on the horizon:

1️ AI-Powered Cyber Attacks

Attackers are already using AI to automate attacks, create deepfake credentials, and even bypass security defenses. Imagine an AI-powered malware that can self-adapt, evade detection, and spread through your entire ICS environment in minutes. Yeah, that's happening.

2️ Supply Chain Attacks on ICS Vendors

Why hack a single factory when you can compromise an entire industry by breaching an ICS hardware vendor? Attackers are targeting software updates, firmware patches, and trusted third-party suppliers to distribute Trojanized malware straight into critical infrastructure.

3️ Quantum Computing Threats

Today's encryption might be secure, but once quantum computers become mainstream, they'll be able to crack even the strongest encryption in seconds. That means every encrypted SCADA system, industrial network, and VPN could suddenly be wide open to attackers.

4️⃣ ICS-Specific Ransomware 2.0

Ransomware gangs are getting more creative and ruthless. Instead of just encrypting data, future ransomware will target PLCs, SCADA controllers, and industrial automation systems—forcing factories to pay up or shut down production entirely.

5️⃣ Rogue 5G and Edge Computing Exploits

With 5G-enabled industrial devices and edge computing taking over, attackers now have even more entry points into ICS/SCADA environments. Expect to see new exploits that take advantage of weakly secured 5G networks and unpatched edge devices in critical infrastructure.

The Future of ICS Security: Challenges We Need to Solve

Security professionals in the ICS/SCADA world already have enough to worry about—but the future brings even bigger challenges. Here's what we need to figure out (and fast):

☐ 1. Bridging the IT-OT Security Gap

Many ICS networks are still running outdated, unpatched legacy systems because "if it ain't broke, don't fix it." But as IT and OT networks continue to merge, we need a better way to integrate security without disrupting operations.

🔒 2. Implementing Zero Trust in ICS Networks

Most industrial networks still operate under the assumption that "inside" traffic is safe. That's a massive mistake. We need to implement Zero Trust security models, where no device, user, or system is trusted by default.

📶 3. Securing Wireless and IIoT Devices

Factories are flooded with wireless sensors, IIoT devices, and real-time monitoring systems. But most of these devices have weak security (or none at all). Without proper authentication, encryption, and monitoring, they'll become prime targets for attackers.

🚀 4. Keeping Up with AI-Driven Threats

As AI becomes a hacking tool, security teams will need to fight AI with AI. That means developing machine learning-based threat detection, automated response systems, and AI-driven security analytics to stay ahead of adaptive cyber threats.

How to Prepare for the Next Generation of ICS Cyber Threats

Security is a moving target—what worked yesterday won't cut it tomorrow. But if you start preparing now, you'll have a much better chance at keeping your industrial environment safe.

✅ **Upgrade to Secure ICS Architectures**

Isolate critical systems from public networks.

Implement network segmentation and air-gapped controls where necessary.

Use Zero Trust principles to limit access based on device behavior and identity.

✅ **Prioritize Security for IIoT and Edge Computing**

Patch vulnerabilities in edge devices before attackers exploit them.

Use secure authentication and encrypted communication for all IIoT devices.

Deploy real-time monitoring to detect suspicious activity.

✅ **Adopt AI and Machine Learning for Cyber Defense**

Use AI-powered security tools for threat detection and anomaly analysis.

Implement behavioral analytics to detect early signs of cyberattacks.

Automate incident response to reduce the damage of fast-moving attacks.

✅ **Prepare for Post-Quantum Cryptography**

Start assessing your encryption strategy now before quantum computing makes it obsolete.

Consider hybrid cryptographic solutions that combine classical and quantum-resistant encryption.

Final Thoughts: The Future of ICS Security is a Warzone

If this chapter gave you mild anxiety, good—that means you're paying attention. The reality is that ICS and SCADA environments are becoming the #1 target for cyberattacks, and the future of industrial security depends on how well we adapt to new threats.

But here's the good news: you're not powerless. The best defense against tomorrow's cyber threats is preparing today.

✓☐ Stay ahead of the latest security trends.
✓☐ Upgrade your defenses before attackers find a way in.
✓☐ Train your team to recognize and respond to cyber threats.

The future doesn't have to be a disaster movie—but only if we start treating cybersecurity as a core part of industrial operations, not an afterthought.

So, let's get to work. Your factory's security depends on it. 🔥💻

Well, folks, we made it! If you've stuck with me through this deep dive into the wild world of Industrial IoT security, congratulations—you now know more about securing smart factories and SCADA systems than most IT professionals (and probably some CISOs, too).

We started by unraveling the chaos of IIoT, understanding why industrial networks are such a mess, and how attackers exploit legacy systems, weak protocols, and unsecured devices. From network segmentation and Zero Trust to firmware hacking, RF security, and cyber-physical exploits, we explored the terrifying yet fascinating reality of securing industrial environments. Along the way, we covered real-world threats like ransomware, insider attacks, and nation-state cyber warfare—because nothing says "fun" like realizing your factory is one misconfigured firewall away from disaster.

But here's the good news: you're now armed with the knowledge to fight back. Whether you're securing a power grid, a manufacturing plant, or a tiny PLC that somehow controls an entire assembly line, you have the strategies to lock down your IIoT systems, monitor for threats, and respond to incidents like a pro. Industrial cybersecurity isn't just about patching vulnerabilities—it's about staying one step ahead of the bad guys, continuously evolving, and making sure your factory doesn't end up as a cautionary tale in the next cybersecurity conference keynote.

A Huge Thank You!

Before I sign off, I want to say a huge THANK YOU to you, my reader. Whether you're a security pro, a hacker, an engineer, or just someone who picked up this book out of curiosity (or mild panic), I appreciate you. Industrial IoT security is complex, ever-changing, and—let's be honest—kind of overwhelming. But the fact that you took the time to learn, explore, and level up your skills? That's awesome.

And if you're craving more hacking adventures, you're in luck. This book is part of the *IoT Red Teaming: Offensive and Defensive Strategies* series, where we explore everything from breaking into smart cars to hacking medical devices and even taking on satellite systems. If you enjoyed this book, you might also like:

- **Mastering Hardware Hacking**: Breaking and Securing Embedded Systems – because nothing screams fun like ripping apart IoT devices and finding hidden backdoors.
- **Wireless Hacking Unleashed**: Attacking Wi-Fi, Bluetooth, and RF Protocols – because wireless networks are basically an open invitation for hackers.

- **Drone Hacking**: Wireless Exploits, GPS Spoofing, and UAV Security – because why hack a factory when you can hijack a drone?
- **AI-Powered IoT Hacking**: Machine Learning Attacks and Defenses – because AI isn't just the future—it's the battleground.

Cybersecurity isn't a one-time thing—it's a continuous battle. So keep learning, keep hacking (ethically, of course), and most importantly, stay paranoid! 🚀

— *Zephyrion Stravos*